THE INSTANT POT® COOKBOOK For Kids

53 Safe, Fun, and Confidence Building Recipes for Your Young Chef

by
Shannon Jett

The Instant Pot® For Kids Cookbook:
53 Safe, Fun, and Confidence Building Recipes for Your Young Chef

Copyright © 2018 Shannon Jett
ISBN: 978-1-945056-53-6
Book Design: Velin@Perseus-Design.com

Back cover: / All photos - Depositphotos.com
zhekos_, stu99, lisovskaya, belchonock

Interior photos: All photos from Depositphotos.com belchonock p. 4, zurijeta p. 4, Odelinde p. 5, monkeybusiness p. 6, SimpleFoto p. 7, monkeybusiness p. 8, anatols p. 10, uriy2007 p. 11, ajafoto p. 12, AEPhotos p. 12, shawn_hempel p. 12, shutswis p. 12, imagedb_seller p. 12, rimglow p. 12, elenathewise p. 12, Vadarshop p. 13, t.r.o.t.z p. 13, kues p. 13, cynoclub p. 13, Bruno135 p. 13, belchonock p. 20, tycoonp. 23, marilyna p. 25, vankad p. 27, HandmadePicture p. 29, Belkantus p. 31, StephanieFrey p. 33, zhekos_ p. 35, bhofack2 p. 39, monkeybusinessp. 41, zoryanchik p. 41, zurijeta p. 43, petrograd99 p. 45, HandmadePicture p. 45, StephanieFrey p. 47, svetas p. 49, mjthp. 50, timolina p. 51, Crisferra p. 53, photosimysia p. 55, svariophoto p. 57, Odelinde p. 59, photominer p. 61, Odelinde p. 63, Odelinde p. 65, rafer76 p. 67, jbryson p. 68, Scruggelgreenp. 69, Seagull_1 p. 71, goceristeski p. 71, manyakotic p. 75, robynmac p. 77, Odelinde p. 79, TeriVirbickis p. 81, mariakarabella p. 83, alisafarov p. 85, tonodiaz p. 87, chasbrutlag p. 85, dehooks p. 87, asimojet p. 89, NoamArmonn p. 91, chasbrutlag p. 93, lenyvavsha p. 95, StephanieFrey p. 97, arskajuhani p. 99, bhofack2 p. 99, photominer p. 101, dar19.30 p. 103, stu99 p. 105, goceristeski p. 106, alexrathsp. 107, lisovskaya p. 111, Syda_Productions p. 112, lenyvavsha p. 113, TarasMalyarevich p. 115, belchonock p. 115, StephanieFrey p. 117, tehcheesiong p. 118, o_ae_1 p. 119, VictoriaAndrea p. 120, Dream79 p. 121, asimojet p. 122, yana-komisarenko@yandex.ru p. 123, NeydtStock p. 125

All rights reserved. The use of any part of this publication reproduced, transmitted in any form or by any means, electronic, mechanical, recording or otherwise, or stored in a retrieval system, without the prior consent of the publisher is an infringement of the copyright law.

In the case of photocopying or other reprographic copying of the material, a license must be obtained before proceeding.

Instant Pot® is the registered trademark of Double Insight Inc., and Instant Pot® was designed in Canada, with healthy living, green living, and ethnic diversity in mind.

Legal Disclaimer

The information contained in this book is the opinion of the author and is based on the author's personal experience and observations. The author does not assume liability whatsoever for the use of or inability to use any or all information contained in this book, and accepts no responsibility for any loss or damages of any kind that may be incurred by the reader as a result of actions arising from the use of information in this book. Use this information at your own risk. The author reserves the right to make any changes he or she deems necessary to future versions of the publication to ensure its accuracy.

CONTENTS

Introduction
A Note To Parents	6
A Note To Kids	8
Getting Started	10
Utensils and Tools	12
Cooking Terms	14
Difficulty Ratings	15
Getting to Know Your Instant Pot®	16

Breakfast
Personal, Kid Sized, Egg, Ham and Cheese Casserole	20
Quack-tastic Hard Boiled Eggs	22
Apple Cinnamon Steel Cut Oats	24
Berry Good Triple Berry Oatmeal	26
Criss Cross Applesauce	28
"Ooh La La!" French Toast Bake	30

Quick Snacks
Cocktail Meatballs	32
Honey Garlic Chicken Wings	34
Buffalo Chicken Dip	36
Spinach Artichoke Dip	38
Hummus is Yummus!	40

Veggies and Side Dishes
Corn-errific Corn on the Cob	42
Blissful & "Bacony" Green Beans	44

Honey Cinnamon Kissed Carrots	46
Acorn Squash with Brown Sugar and Butter	48
Mashed Potatoes, Not Couch Potatoes	50
3,2,1 Blast Off Rice Pilaf	52
Cheesy Vegetable Risotto	54
Princess and the Split Pea Soup	56

Lunch

Chicken Corn Chowder	58
Creamy Dreamy Tomato Soup	60
Chicken Salad Sandwiches	62
Baked Potato Heads	64
Macaroni and Cheese, Please!	66
Step Right Up, Get Yer Hot Dogs!	68

Dinner

Poultry

Chicken Tacos (Dragon Approved)	70
Cheesy Stuffed Chicken in Alfredo Sauce	72
Sweet and Sassy Honey Chicken	74
Rosemary Lemon "Big Ole" Whole Chicken	76
Pineapple Chicken "That's Just Maui Messin' Around"	78
BBQ Chicken Sliders	80
Presto Pesto Chicken Packets	82
Chicken Noodle "Sick Day" Soup	84

Beef

Sloppy Joe, Slop Sloppy Joe	86
Willy Nilly Chili	88
"Knock Your Socks Off" Beef Stroganoff	90
Spaghetti	92
Magnificent Meatloaf Muffins	94
Big Kid Beef and Broccoli	96

Pork

Country Style Boneless Pork Ribs	98
Pulled Pork in BBQ Sauce	100
Pork Tenderloin in Balsamic Apple Sauce	102
"You Can Be a Big Pig, Too" Kalua Pork	104
Baby Back Ribs	106

Seafood

Lemon Snickety Salmon	108
Peel-and-Eat Shrimp	110
Shrimp Jambalaya (Have Big Fun On The Bayou!)	112

Desserts

Volcano Chocolate Lava Cakes	114
Awesome Apple Dumplings	116
Oreo Cheesecake	118
Easy Breezy Peach Pie	120
Fudgy Peanut Butter Brownies	122
"Monkeying Around" Monkey Bread	124
Index	126

A NOTE TO PARENTS

Hi there! As a parent myself, I know how much fun it can be to have my kids helping in the kitchen. I want to encourage their love of food and creating and let's face it…kids are much more willing to try new things if they have been involved in the creative process. But it can also be a challenge to find recipes that are healthy, appetizing and well-written. Most kids are just learning the basics and need detailed step-by-step instructions to guide them through a recipe.

You may be asking yourself, "Why the Instant Pot®? Is it safe enough for my child to handle?" I asked those same questions as I did my research. I saw plenty of kids' cookbooks that involve the oven and stovetop. I've used the Instant Pot®

for many years now, and personally, I feel like the Instant Pot® is safer and easier than a stove or oven for a novice chef. It's also less likely that food is going to be burned or ruined, which means your little chef will have a high success rate.

As I put this book together, I involved my two young girls, ages 5 and 7, in the process. We cooked, created and sampled. They enjoyed the tried and true recipes like Spaghetti and Macaroni and Cheese and loved branching out and trying new favorites, such as Princess and the Split Pea Soup and BBQ Chicken Sliders.

I tried to make this book well rounded and included everything from breakfast to dessert and even a few snack ideas. Every kid should be able to find plenty of recipes that pique their interest. And I've found that kids are usually willing to sample their own cooking, even if they normally would never try Cheesy Vegetable Risotto.

While this book is written with very detailed instructions, it is still best to be present in the kitchen or at least available if extra help is needed. Younger children will need a little closer supervision, while older children may just need occasional help. Because of the nature of the Instant Pot®, most of these recipes are for full meals that your whole family can enjoy. The majority of the recipes make about 4-6 servings although a few make more and are wonderful as leftovers. Several of the breakfast and dessert recipes only make 1-2 servings but can easily be doubled.

I hope you and your kids enjoy sharing this special time and that they gain knowledge and independence as they become more confident in the kitchen. Wishing you and your family many happy meals!

A NOTE TO KIDS

I'm so glad you are excited to learn about cooking! Cooking and creating yummy foods in the kitchen is so much fun and super tasty. You will be able to prepare all of your favorite foods as well as play with new foods you may not have tried before. Who knows, you may find a new favorite!

Why is cooking important? Well, of course, everyone has to eat. And wouldn't you rather eat something that is really yummy than just a boring ole' sandwich? Learning to cook now is a skill that will serve you for your entire life. You'll be able to impress your family and friends by serving up tasty dishes that will make them feel loved and appreciated.

This book has a bunch of recipes that have been approved by other kids. Not only are there the basic recipes that most kids love, but I'm sure you will find some new favorite things to try. Don't be afraid to branch out and try new recipes or foods you've never had. That's part of the adventure and you may love it!

I'm sure you already have an Instant Pot® and have seen your grown-ups use it to make dinner or other fun treats. The Instant Pot® helps to make meals that taste great and get to the table fast. Now it's your turn to try. The Instant Pot® is safe and easy to use if you follow the directions in this book.

This recipe collection has easy recipes if you are just starting out and more complex recipes for the more advanced chef. Although kids can do a lot of the cooking themselves, you may need to ask an adult to help you sometimes and that's okay. They can be your assistant and maybe they will even help you do the dishes when you are done cooking!

GETTING STARTED

It's best to start a new recipe by reading through the entire recipe. You may find helpful tips that will make your recipe a success. Then it's a good idea to put on an apron to protect your clothes from spills. Plus, it makes you look like a real chef! Wash your hands and you are ready to get started.

Each recipe has the name of the recipe and a little bit about it, followed by how many servings it makes. It is important to know how many people you are serving so you know if the recipe will make enough food for everyone.

Next you will find the list of ingredients. I find that it is most convenient to go ahead and gather all of your ingredients together. Wash and safely chop up any vegetables, gather all the spices and make sure your meat is not frozen and is ready to cook. Some recipes come together fast and you don't want to worry about burning something while you are trying to find a missing ingredient.

The next section lists any important tools you may need. Most of these tools are specific tools that are made for the Instant Pot®, such as the trivet and small cooking dishes. It's always helpful to have oven mitts as sometimes the food and pans are hot. Gather these helpful tools so they are easy to reach when you need them.

Now you are ready to follow the step-by-step directions and create some yummy food!

UTENSILS AND TOOLS

Tricks of the Trade

What's a whisk and what's the difference between minced and chopped? How much is a pinch of salt? Cooking is sometimes a language all its own and it is important to know what the lingo means. This section will break down all the terms to make it easy for you to follow a recipe.

Baking Dish

a glass, ceramic or metal dish that can withstand the heat of the oven.

Baking Sheet

a large metal tray that can be placed in the oven. Most have a small 1-inch rim around the outside of the tray to prevent any food from spilling into the oven.

Colander

a large bowl filled with holes used to drain the liquid from food, such as pasta. Also handy for washing fruits and vegetables.

Food Processor

an electric appliance similar to a blender. It can be used to finely chop and blend food items together.

Ladle

a large "spoon" that is more like a deep bowl attached to a long handle. Helpful for serving soups or scooping liquid as it holds more than a big spoon does.

Measuring Cup

a large cup, that is used for measuring ingredients.

Measuring Spoons

usually sized in teaspoons and tablespoons, these are used to measure ingredients when cooking.

Ramekin

small oven proof bowls used for making and serving individual portions.

Springform Pan

a round cake pan with 3 inch sides. The side has a spring loaded clasp that allows the bottom to be removed from the side. Ideal for making cheesecakes and other desserts with thick batter.

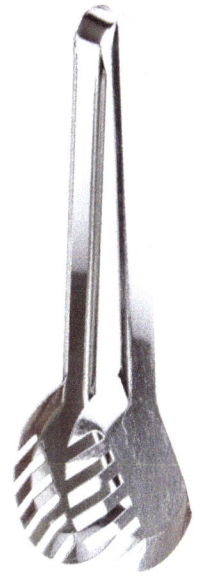

Tongs

long handled tool used to assist in gripping food. A handy tool for turning meat or removing food from a hot pot.

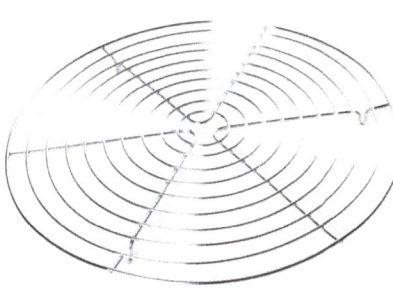

Trivet

the wire rack that came with your Instant Pot® that can be used at the bottom of the pot to keep food or dishes out of the liquid at the bottom.

Whisk

a wire kitchen tool used for blending and mixing food. Because of its design, a whisk is handy for eliminating food lumps and incorporating air into a mixture while stirring.

COOKING TERMS

Boiling - occurs at high heat when a liquid bubbles up powerfully.

Broiling - uses an oven to expose food to very high heat. Best for crisping or browning food just before serving. Most foods only need to broil for a few minutes and can burn easily if left in too long.

Chop - to cut food pieces, such a vegetables, fruits or meats into smaller pieces. Chopped pieces tend to be a little larger and less precise than diced pieces.

Core - to cut and remove the core of fruit, such as an apple.

Dice - to cut food, such as vegetables, fruit or meat into really small uniform pieces.

Grate - using a device to transform large pieces into much smaller, finer pieces. Can be used for cheese, spices, vegetables and fruits.

Mince - to cut food into very tiny, fine pieces.

Peel - use a vegetable peeler or sharp knife to remove the skin from fruits or vegetables.

Pinch - a very small amount of something, usually referring to seasoning. To add a pinch of something, for example salt, add a small amount of salt into the palm of your hand. Use your thumb and index fingers to "pinch" a small amount of the salt and sprinkle it into your recipe.

Simmer - to allow liquid placed over high heat to bubble slightly as it cooks. Simmering should bubble with less force than an item that is boiling.

Sauté - to brown or cook food in a small amount of fat or oil using high heat. The food is cooked quickly and often develops a browned area just on the surface.

DIFFICULTY RATINGS

I have rated each recipe using 1, 2, or 3 pots to let you know how much work will go into it.

 These are the simplest recipes. You can cook most of these recipes by just dumping the ingredients into the pot and turning it on!

 Two pot recipes usually require a bit of chopping, peeling and mixing. Some recipes will include using the "Saute" feature on your Instant Pot®.

 Most of the three pot recipes include longer ingredient lists, longer prep times and more involved cooking. These are good recipes to have an adult around to help you if you in case you need it.

GETTING TO KNOW YOUR INSTANT POT®

At first glance the Instant Pot® can look kind of intimidating. All those buttons! But it is really pretty simple once you get the hang of it.

The Instant Pot® is an electric pressure cooker that uses the steam that builds when the lid is secure to cook the food quickly. There are three main parts to get to know on your electric pressure cooker.

Lid - The lid locks into place and prevents the steam from escaping while it is cooking. It also has a safety mechanism to prevent

you from removing the lid when the pot has too much pressure. This protects you from messy, and perhaps dangerous mishaps in the kitchen.

The lid has a moveable valve on it. The valve has two options. Sealed position is when the pot is sealed and able to come to pressure and cook your food. The other option is venting, where the pot is open and releasing the pressure that was built.

The lid also has a silver float valve, that looks like a small silver button. When the pot has reached pressure and is cooking food, the silver float valve will be up. When the pot is not at pressure, the silver valve is down.

Inner Pot - The inner pot is the place where you will put your cooking ingredients and actually cook the food. It is stainless steel and dishwasher safe.

Body - This is the big thing with all the buttons! The plug is located on the body as well as the panel with the buttons you will use for cooking.

There are a few main buttons that you will need to know.

The **"Manual"** button is the most commonly used button in the book. It cooks at high pressure.

Use the **"Sauté"** button to heat the bottom of the pot to high heat quickly to brown or sauté food before cooking.

The **"+"** and **"-"** are used to adjust cooking time durations.

The **"Pressure"** key adjusts high to low pressure cooking.

The **"Keep Warm/Cancel"** function is used to stop the cooking process when the pressure cooker is programmed. It can also be used for keeping the food warm before serving.

The **"Soup"** button is used to cook soup, of course! It cooks at high pressure.

Some "Technical" Terms

Cooking with the Instant Pot® definitely has a vocabulary of its own. Here are some tips to help you understand the directions for each recipe.

"Make sure the steam valve is in the closed or sealed position." This means to flip the valve on the lid so that your food can cook.

"Adjust the timer." Use the "+" or "—" key to add more or less minutes according to your directions.

"Quick release" When the timer beeps, flip open the valve on the lid to venting to release all the steam and pressure. *Be careful!!!* The steam that comes out is hot.

"Natural release" When the timer beeps and the recipe calls for a natural release, don't open the steam vent. This allows the food to cook just a bit longer as the pot cools down and releases the pressure on its own.

As you start cooking, always remember that for the pressure cooker to work, you must have at least one cup of liquid in the inner pot for it to come to pressure.

Building a Sling

A sling is helpful when you are cooking with a separate pot or dish inside the inner pot. It can be too hot to touch with your hands and hard to get out, so a sling is necessary and easy to make with a strip of aluminum foil.

1. Cut a strip of aluminum foil about 18-20 inches long.
2. Fold the aluminum foil in half lengthwise.
3. Fold it in half lengthwise one more time.
4. Voilà! You have a sling and are ready to get cookin'!
5. Just put it underneath any pot or dish that you put inside the main inner pot of the pressure cooker so that you can pull that dish out by holding the sling instead of the hot dish.

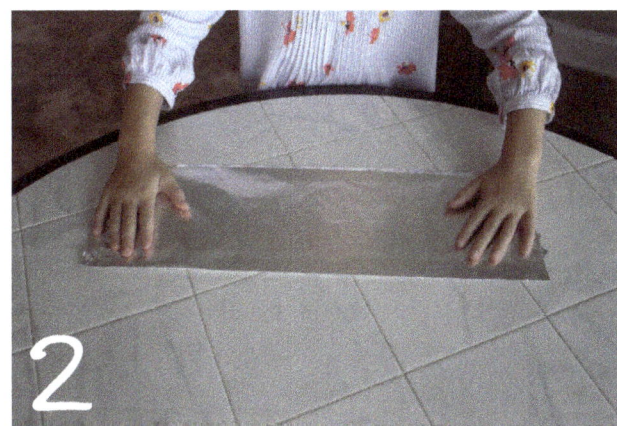

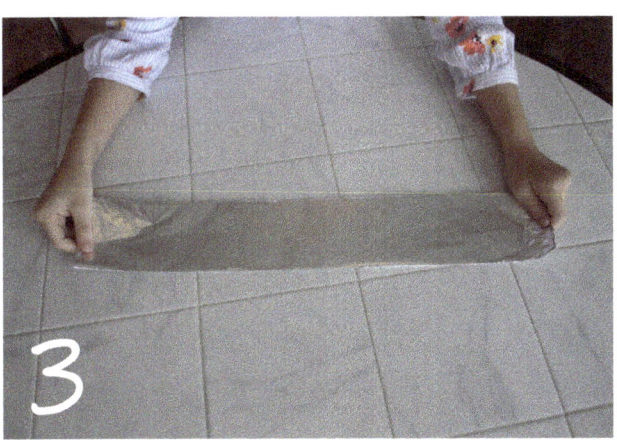

PERSONAL, KID SIZED, EGG, HAM AND CHEESE CASSEROLE

Get your day off to a great start with a delicious breakfast! Eggs are full of protein that will fuel your body until lunchtime. You can even substitute cooked sausage for the ham if that's what you like better.

Serves: Two 6-ounce ramekins

What You Need:
- 3 eggs
- 1 tablespoon milk
- 1/4 cup shredded cheese (a mix of cheddar and mozzarella is great, but use whatever you like)
- 4-6 tablespoons diced ham
- Pinch of salt and ground black pepper
- 2 cups water (for bottom of the Inner Pot)

Tools:
- Two 6-ounce Ramekins
- Trivet
- Cooking spray

Breakfast

How You Make It:

1 Gently crack the eggs into a medium sized mixing bowl. Add the milk. Use your fingers to add a pinch of salt and pepper. Using a whisk, beat the eggs until they are well mixed.

2 Add the cheese to the eggs and mix.

3 Coat the ramekin bowls with cooking spray, being sure to get the sides as well as the bottom. Scoop 2-3 tablespoons of diced ham into each bowl.

4 Divide the egg mixture into the two bowls, being sure each bowl gets some of the cheesy goodness. Stir gently to mix the ham, but be careful not to splash the egg out of the bowl. Each ramekin should be about 3/4 full. The eggs will expand so don't overfill.

5 Add the trivet to the inner pot of your Instant Pot®. Pour 2 cups of water into the bottom. Carefully add the ramekins to the pot and set them on the trivet.

6 Close the lid securely and make sure the steam vent is in the closed position.

7 Press the "Manual" button and adjust the timer to 8 minutes.

8 When the timer beeps after 8 minutes, turn the steam vent and release the pressure carefully.

9 Use oven mitts to pull each ramekin out of the inner pot. Eat them straight out of the bowl or turn them upside down on a plate. Delicious!

Tip for Success

Here's how to measure a pinch of an ingredient. Pour just a little into the palm of your hand. Use the tips of your fingers to "pinch" the ingredients. Sprinkle the pinch into your bowl and discard the rest in the sink or trash can.

Tasty Tip

Make your egg casserole extra healthy by adding a few tablespoons of your favorite chopped veggies. Tomatoes, mushrooms and spinach are all egg-cellent choices!

QUACK-TASTIC HARD BOILED EGGS

Hard boiled eggs make a delicious breakfast or snack. This is also a great way to get all of your eggs ready when dying Easter eggs. And no one eats 5 dozen eggs a day like Gaston!

Serves: Makes 6 hard boiled eggs

What You Need:
- 6 eggs
- 2 cups water (for bottom of the Instant Pot®)

Tools:
- Trivet or Steamer Basket
- Tongs
- Large bowl of Ice Water

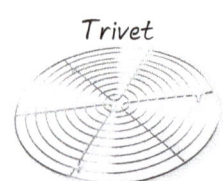
Trivet

Tongs

How You Make It:

1 Pour 2 cups of water into the inner pot of the Instant Pot®. Put a trivet or steamer basket into the pot.

2 Gently place the eggs into the basket or trivet. Close the lid. Make sure the steam vent is in the closed position.

3 Press the "Manual" button and set the timer for 6 minutes.

4 When the timer beeps after 6 minutes, let the pressure release naturally for another 6 minutes. Then flip the steam vent to open and release the remaining pressure.

5 Open the lid. Using tongs, carefully transfer the eggs to a bowl of ice water. This will stop the eggs from cooking any more.

6 Peel and eat your eggs and store any leftover eggs in the refrigerator.

Breakfast

APPLE CINNAMON STEEL CUT OATS

This is the perfect breakfast for a cool fall morning, or any morning really. Delicious steel cut oats are always a healthy breakfast choice, but adding the apples and cinnamon makes them extra tasty.

Serves: 1

What You Need:
- 1/4 cup steel cut oats
- 1/2 apple, peeled, cored and diced into small pieces
- 3/4 cup water
- 1/2 teaspoon ground cinnamon
- 1-2 teaspoons brown sugar
- pinch of nutmeg
- 2 cups water (for the bottom of the Inner Pot)

Tools:
- Heat-Proof Cooking Bowl
- Trivet
- Oven mitt

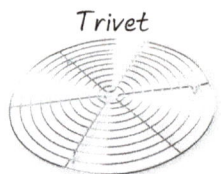
Trivet

How You Make It:

1. In a heat-proof bowl that fits inside your Instant Pot®, mix together all the ingredients except the two cups of water.

2. Place 2 cups of water into the bottom of the inner pot of the Instant Pot®. Set the trivet in the pot.

3. Place the bowl with the oat mixture on top of the trivet. Secure the lid and close the steam vent.

Breakfast

4 Press the "Manual" button and set the cook time for 15 minutes.

5 When the timer beeps after 15 minutes, allow the pressure to release naturally. This will take about another 15 minutes.

6 When the silver float valve has dropped down you may remove the lid. Use oven mitts to carefully lift the bowl of oats out of the Instant Pot®.

7 Stir and add any additional sweetness or a little milk if desired.

8 Enjoy your yummy breakfast!

BERRY GOOD TRIPLE BERRY OATMEAL

The berries add so much sweetness to this oatmeal that you will think you are eating dessert! Although the recipe calls for berries, any mixture of frozen fruit will do.

Serves: 2

What You Need:
- 1/3 cup rolled oats
- 2/3 cup water
- 1/2 cup frozen mixed berries
- pinch of cinnamon
- 2 cups water (for bottom of the Inner Pot)

Tools:
- Trivet
- Ramekin or Heat Proof Mug or Bowl

Ramekin   Trivet

How You Make It:

1 Pour 2 cups of water into the bottom of the inner pot of the pressure cooker. Place the trivet in the pot.

2 In a ramekin or heat proof bowl, mix together the rolled oats, water and a pinch of cinnamon. Add the frozen berries to the top.

3 Place the bowl into the pot on top of the trivet. Close the lid. Place the steam valve in the sealed position.

4 Press the "Manual" button and adjust the timer to 10 minutes.

5 When the cook time is completed, allow the pressure to release naturally. This will take about another 10 minutes.

Breakfast

6 When the silver valve has dropped down, it is safe to remove the lid. Use an oven mitt to carefully lift the oatmeal bowl out of the pot.

7 Stir the berries into the oatmeal and enjoy!

Tasty Tip
Mush a few of the berries with a spoon and stir into the oatmeal to create purple oatmeal that tastes delicious! You can double or triple this recipe without adding any additional cooking time. Just be sure to do each serving in its own little bowl.

CRISS CROSS APPLESAUCE

Homemade applesauce tastes way better than the kind you buy in the store. The Instant Pot® makes it super easy for you to make it in your own kitchen.

Serves: 4-6 servings

What You Need:
- 8 apples, peeled, cored and cut into quarters
- 1 cup water
- 2 tablespoons brown sugar (optional)
- 1 teaspoon cinnamon (optional)

How You Make It:

1. Peel all the apples and cut them into four pieces. Remove the cores and seeds. Place the apple chunks into the Instant Pot®.

2. Pour in the 1 cup of water. Add the sugar and cinnamon if you are using them.

3. Close the lid. Make sure to close the steam vent.

4. Press the "Manual" button and set the timer for 8 minutes.

5. When the timer beeps after 8 minutes, allow the pressure to release naturally. When the silver valve drops down, you can open your Instant Pot®. If you open it right away you will wind up with a big mess!

6. Stir your apple sauce and let it cool before serving up a big bowl. Keep leftovers in a sealed container in the refrigerator.

Breakfast

Tip for Success

You can use whatever type of apple you like. We love the tanginess of the Granny Smith apples, but many people love the sweetness of a Gala or Fuji apple. Mix and Match!

"OOH LA LA!" FRENCH TOAST BAKE

The perfect breakfast for Saturday morning and the perfect use of bread that is slightly stale.

Serves: 4

What You Need:
- 7 slices of french bread, cut into cubes
- 2 eggs
- 1/2 cup milk
- 2 tablespoons brown sugar
- 2 teaspoons vanilla extract
- 1 teaspoon cinnamon
- Cooking Spray

For topping:
- Chocolate Chips
- Maple Syrup
- Diced Fruit
- Pecans

Tools:
- Trivet
- Whisk
- 7 Inch Round Baking Dish
- Oven Mitts
- Oven, Preheated to Broil (optional)

How You Make It:

1 Pour 2 cups of water into the bottom of the inner pot of the pressure cooker. Place the trivet into the pot.

2 In a large mixing bowl, beat together the eggs and the milk. Add the brown sugar, cinnamon, and vanilla extract and mix well. Add the cubes of bread to the mixture and use a spoon to mix, covering the bread with the liquid.

3 Coat the inside if your 7 inch baking dish with cooking spray. Pour the now soggy bread cubes into the baking dish.

4 Place the baking dish onto the trivet in the Instant Pot® and close the lid. Be sure the steam vent is in the sealed position.

Breakfast

5 Press the "Manual" button and set the timer for 15 minutes.

6 When the timer beeps after 15 minutes, allow the pressure to release for another 5 minutes. Then open the steam vent to release remaining pressure.

7 Use oven mitts to carefully remove the baking dish from the pot. It will be hot!

8 If you would like the top of the french toast to be crunchy, place the baking dish into a preheated oven. Broil for 3-5 minutes. Check it frequently so it doesn't burn.

9 Scoop the french toast onto plates and serve with your favorite toppings!

COCKTAIL MEATBALLS

Cocktail meatballs are a crowd pleaser for both kids and grown-ups. Help prepare for your next party or just fix an extra tasty snack.

Serves: 8-10 as an appetizer

What You Need:
- 1 bag (3-4 pounds) frozen meatballs
- 1 can (14 ounce) jellied cranberry sauce
- 1 (12 ounce) jar Chili sauce
- 1 cup water

Tools:
- Cooking Spray
- Steamer Basket
- Toothpicks

How You Make It:

1. Add 1 cup of water to the inner pot and place the steamer basket inside.

2. Fill the steamer basket up with the frozen meatballs.

3. Close the lid and make sure the steam valve is in the sealed position.

4. Press the "Manual" button and set the timer for 5 minutes.

5. When the timer beeps after 5 minutes, flip the steam valve carefully to release the pressure.

6. Remove the steamer basket with the meatballs. Drain the water from the inner pot and put the pot back in the Instant Pot®.

7. Spray the inside of the inner pot of your Instant Pot® with cooking spray. This will make clean-up easier later.

8. Press the "Sauté" button and add the cranberry sauce and chili sauce to the pot. Use a spatula to break the cranberry sauce into smaller pieces. Stir frequently until the cranberry sauce chunks have dissolved. The sauce should be smooth.

Quick Snacks

9 Add the cooked meatballs back to the pot and stir to coat in the sauce. Press the "Keep Warm/Cancel" button so the pot will keep your meatballs warm for serving.

10 Serve your meatballs with toothpicks.

HONEY GARLIC CHICKEN WINGS

Unlike some chicken wings that are super spicy, these wings are cooked in a mild, but flavorful sauce. Adjust the amount of crushed red pepper flakes according to how spicy you like your wings.

Serves: 4-8 (Makes 4 pounds of wings)

What You Need:
- 4 pounds chicken wings, patted dry
- 1/2 cup honey
- 1/3 cup low sodium soy sauce
- 5 teaspoons garlic, minced
- 1 teaspoon freshly grated ginger or 1/8 teaspoon ground ginger
- 1/2 teaspoon crushed red pepper flakes (more if you like things spicy, less if you don't like spicy foods at all)

Tools:
- Cooking Spray
- Tongs
- Baking Sheet
- Oven (optional)
- Basting Brush or Spoon

Tongs

How You Make It:

1 Pat the wings dry using paper towels. Spray the inner pot of the pressure cooker with cooking spray. Add the wings to the pot.

2 In a mixing bowl, stir together the honey, soy sauce, garlic, ginger and red pepper flakes. Pour the sauce over the chicken.

3 Secure the lid and close the steam vent. Press the "Manual" button and set the timer to 5 minutes.

4 If you are going to make the chicken wings crispy in the oven, now is a good time to pre-heat the oven to broil.

5 When the pressure cooker cook time is complete, allow the pressure to release naturally for 10 minutes before opening the steam vent.

Quick Snacks

6 Open the lid and use tongs to remove the chicken wings from the pot and place them on a baking sheet. If you are going to bake them to crisp them up, place them under the oven broiler for about 2-3 minutes. If you don't want to broil them, just set them aside.

7 Press the "Sauté" button on the Instant Pot® and bring the sauce in the pot to a simmer. Simmer, stirring often for 5-7 minutes, or until sauce has thickened.

8 Use a basting brush or spoon to brush the wings with the sauce and serve. Serve with extra sauce on the side.

BUFFALO CHICKEN DIP

This is our favorite dip to serve when we have guests. It's super easy to make, but tastes like you spent a long time in the kitchen. Even though it is buffalo flavored, it only has mild spiciness, so most kids and parents seem to love it.

Serves: 6-8

What You Need:
- 1 pound boneless, skinless chicken breasts
- 1 packet ranch dip seasoning
- 1 cup Buffalo hot sauce
- 1 (8 ounce) stick butter
- 1 (8 ounce) cream cheese
- 2 cups shredded cheddar cheese

Tools:
- Cooking Spray
- Whisk

Whisk

How You Make It:

1 Spray the inner pot of the pressure cooker with cooking spray to prevent the food from sticking.

2 Add the butter, chicken, hot sauce, ranch seasoning, and cream cheese to the pot.

3 Secure the lid and make sure the steam vent is sealed. Press the "Manual" button and set the timer for 15 minutes.

4 When the timer beeps after 15 minutes, quick release the pressure by carefully opening the steam vent.

Quick Snacks

5 Use two forks to shred the chicken. It may be easier to place the chicken on a plate or in a large bowl to shred.

6 Use a whisk and stir the other ingredients. Whisk in the cheese until it has melted. Add the shredded chicken back to the pot and stir.

7 Serve with corn chips, pita chips or sliced veggies.

SPINACH ARTICHOKE DIP

With this cheesy dip, you won't even notice you are eating healthy spinach! I like to chop the artichokes prior to adding them to the dip. This helps distribute the artichoke flavor throughout the whole dish.

Serves: 6

What You Need:
- 1 tablespoon minced garlic
- 1/2 cup chicken broth
- 1 (14 ounce) can or jar of artichoke hearts, drained and chopped
- 10 ounces frozen spinach
- 8 ounces cream cheese
- 1/2 cup mayonnaise
- 1/2 cup sour cream
- 1 (0.7 ounce) packet Italian Dressing Seasoning Mix (optional)
- 6 ounces shredded Parmesan Cheese

Tools:
- Baking Dish

Baking dish

How You Make It:

1 Drain the artichoke hearts from the liquid inside the jar. Using a knife, carefully chop the artichokes into smaller pieces.

2 Press the "Sauté" button on the Instant Pot® and add the minced garlic to the pot. Cook for one minute, then pour the chicken broth into the pot. Press the "Keep Warm/ Cancel" button.

3 Add the chopped artichokes, frozen spinach, cream cheese, mayonnaise, sour cream and Italian Dressing seasoning to the pot. Do not stir.

4 Secure the lid and be sure the steam valve is in the closed position.

Quick Snack

5 Press the "Manual" button and set the timer for 4 minutes. When the cook time is complete, open the steam valve to quick release the pressure.

6 Stir the dip inside the pot to blend the ingredients. Stir the cheese in until it has melted.

7 Transfer the dip to a serving bowl and serve with tortilla chips or chopped raw veggies.

HUMMUS IS YUMMUS!

Store bought hummus is great, but if you are looking to up the flavor, try making your own hummus. Your Instant Pot® will make sure the garbanzo beans are perfectly cooked, so all you will have to do is blend together the remaining ingredients. Easy, peasy!

Serves: 6

What You Need:
(To prepare garbanzo beans)
- 1 pound dried garbanzo beans
- 12 cups water

(To prepare hummus)
- 3 cups of the cooked garbanzo beans, still warm
- 1/2 cup liquid the beans were cooked in
- 1/4 cup tahini
- 2 cloves of garlic
- 1 large lemon, juiced
- 1 teaspoon salt
- 1/2 teaspoon ground cumin
- 1/4 teaspoon smoked paprika
- 1/4 cup extra virgin olive oil

Tools:
- Strainer or Colander
- Food Processor

Colander

How You Make It:

1 Sort through the dried garbanzo beans and remove any stones or wilted beans. Rinse the beans and add into the inner pot of your pressure cooker. Pour 12 cups of water into the pot.

2 Close the lid and be sure the steam valve is in the sealed position. Press the "Manual" button and set the timer for 35 minutes.

3 When the cooking time is complete, allow the pressure to release naturally until the silver float valve has dropped. This could take up to 30 minutes.

4 Open the lid and use a strainer or colander to drain the water from the beans. Reserve about 3/4 cups of the liquid.

Quick Snacks

5 Measure out three cups of the cooked beans and add into the bowl of a food processor. Add all of the remaining ingredients except for the olive oil.

6 Turn on the food processor and blend the ingredients until smooth and creamy. Slowly add the olive oil, about 1 tablespoon at a time, until desired creaminess is reached.

7 Scoop into a serving bowl and serve with veggies, crackers or pita bread.

8 Store in an air-tight container in the refrigerator.

Tip for Success

One pound of garbanzo beans will yield about 9 cups of cooked beans. Store the remaining beans and some of the reserved cooking liquid to have on hand to cook hummus another time. Divide the beans into two remaining servings and freeze with the cooking liquid. Now you can prepare hummus whenever the craving strikes!

CORN-ERRIFIC CORN ON THE COB

There are lots of ways to prepare corn on the cob, but our family's favorite way is using the Instant Pot®. You can help prepare dinner by shucking and cooking the corn until it is juicy and steaming. Yum!

Serves: 4

What You Need:
- 4 fresh ears of corn, shucked
- Butter
- Salt and pepper
- 2 cups water (for bottom of the Inner Pot)

Tools:
- Trivet
- Tongs

Tongs

Trivet

How You Make It:

1. Remove the corn husks from the corn, being sure to get all the silk tassels. Discard the husks and give the corn a quick rinse in the sink.

2. Pour 2 cups of water into the inner pot and place the trivet in the pot. Add the corn on top of the trivet.

3. Close the lid securely. Place the steam valve in the closed position.

4. Press the "Manual" button and set the timer for 2 minutes.

5. When the timer beeps after 2 minutes, open the steam vent to quick release the pressure.

6. Use tongs to carefully remove the hot corn. Place it in a large bowl or on a plate.

7. Serve with butter, salt and pepper.

Veggies and Side Dishes

BLISSFUL & "BACONY" GREEN BEANS

Preparing fresh green beans is a good skill to have. Not only are they full of vitamins and good for you, they taste delicious. Instant Pot® green beans are the best!

Serves: 4

What You Need:
- 1 pound of green beans, ends trimmed and cut in half
- 4 strips bacon
- 1/4 cup of diced white onion (if you like them)
- 2 teaspoons olive oil
- 1/4 teaspoon garlic powder
- 1/8 teaspoon salt
- 1/8 teaspoon ground black pepper
- 2 cups water (for bottom of the Inner Pot)

Tools:
- Trivet or Steamer Basket
- Tongs

How You Make It:

1 Wash and trim your green beans. Discard any that look wrinkled or yucky and then use your fingers to pinch off the very ends of the good green beans.

2 Use kitchen scissors to cut the bacon into 1/2 inch pieces.

3 Press the "Sauté" button on the Instant Pot® and add the bacon to the inner pot. If you are using onion, add the onion, too. Sauté the bacon and onion until the bacon is cooked and the onion has softened. Scoop the bacon and onion mixture into a small bowl or onto a plate and set aside.

4 Press the "Keep Warm/ Cancel" button on the Instant Pot®. Pour 2 cups of water into the inner pot. Place in the trivet or steamer basket. Add the green beans on top of the trivet or basket.

5 Drizzle the olive oil onto the green beans and sprinkle in the salt, ground pepper and garlic powder.

Veggies and Side Dishes

6. Place the lid on the pot and secure. Close the steam valve so no steam can escape.

7. Press the "Manual" button and adjust the timer so the green beans cook for 4 minutes.

8. When the timer beeps after 4 minutes, flip the steam valve carefully to release the pressure.

9. Remove the steamer basket or use tongs to scoop the green beans into a bowl. With the green beans in a serving bowl, add the bacon and onion mixture and mix gently to combine.

10. Serve proudly!

HONEY CINNAMON KISSED CARROTS

Who gets excited about carrots? Trust me, this recipe tastes less like carrots, and more like candy. And have you heard that eating carrots is good for your eyes? That's because carrots are full of vitamin A, which is essential for good eyesight. Eating your carrots will NOT be a chore with this sweet recipe.

Serves: 6

What You Need:
- 2 pounds baby carrots
- 1/2 cup water
- 1 1/2 teaspoons salt (divided)
- 2 tablespoons butter, melted
- 1/4 cup honey
- 1/4 teaspoon vanilla extract
- 1 teaspoon ground cinnamon

How You Make It:

1. Add the carrots into the inner pot of the pressure cooker. Stir together the water and 1 teaspoon of salt. Pour on top of the carrots.

2. Secure the lid and close the steam vent. Press the "Manual" button and set the timer for 3 minutes.

3. While the carrots cook, mix together the butter, honey, vanilla and cinnamon in a small bowl.

4. When the carrot's cooking time is complete, flip the steam vent open to release the pressure.

5. Drain the water from the pot. Stir in the butter and honey mixture, stirring to coat all the carrots.

6. Season to taste with remaining salt and serve.

Veggies and Side Dishes

Tip for Success

Cook your carrots for 3 minutes, unless you like them still a little crunchy. Then cook them for only 2 minutes.

ACORN SQUASH WITH BROWN SUGAR AND BUTTER

Acorn squash makes the perfect side dish in the fall. It's so sweet and fun to eat. Do yourself a favor and give this one a try!

Serves: 2

What You Need:
- 1 medium acorn squash, cut in half
- 2 tablespoons brown sugar
- 2 tablespoons butter, melted
- 2 tablespoons maple syrup
- 2 pinches salt

Tools:
- Trivet
- Tongs

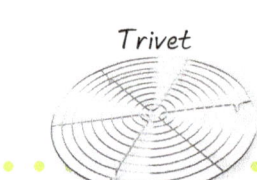

How You Make It:

1 Cut the acorn squash in half and scoop out the seeds with a metal spoon.

2 Mix together in a small bowl the melted butter with the brown sugar. Pour in the maple syrup and add a few pinches of salt. Mix with a spoon until well combined.

3 Use a spoon to drizzle the the brown sugar butter mixture onto the inside of the squash. Use your fingers to rub the mixture all over the inside, coating equally.

4 Pour 1 cup of water into the inner pot of the pressure cooker. Place the trivet in the pot.

5 Put the acorn squash on top of the trivet with the skin facing down and the brown sugar butter side facing up.

6 Secure the lid and be sure the steam vent is closed. Press the "Manual" button and adjust the cook time to 5 minutes.

Veggies and Side Dishes

7 When the cook time is complete and the timer beeps, allow the pressure to release naturally for another 5 minutes. Then flip open the steam vent and release the remaining pressure.

8 Use tongs to remove the pieces of squash from the pot. Set onto a plate to cool slightly before serving.

MASHED POTATOES, NOT COUCH POTATOES

Making your own mashed potatoes is easier than it may seem. These potatoes are a delicious side dish that you can make for dinner for your family. For some extra fun, top with shredded cheese or bacon bits.

Serves: 4

What You Need:
- 1 1/2 pounds Yukon Gold potatoes
- 1/2 teaspoon salt
- 4 tablespoons heavy whipping cream
- 2 tablespoons butter
- 1 tablespoon milk

Tools:
- Colander
- Potato Masher

Colander

How You Make It:

1 Peel the potatoes and cut them into quarters (each potato into 4 pieces).

2 Add the potatoes to your Instant Pot® and add water so they are just covered. Add the salt and stir gently, just to dissolve the salt.

3 Close the lid and be sure the steam vent is in the sealed position.

4 Press the "Manual" button and set the cook time for 10 minutes.

Veggies and Side Dishes

Tasty Tip
Looking for something fun to serve at a party or just to spice up your dinner routine? Try making a mashed potato bar! Set out a variety of toppings and serve the potatoes in fancy glasses. Let your guests or family dress their potatoes with all of their favorite toppings. Yummy!

5. When the timer beeps, carefully open the steam vent to release the pressure. Use a colander to drain the water from the potatoes.

6. With the potatoes back in the Instant Pot®, use your masher to immediately mash them up. Make them as smooth or as chunky as you like!

7. Mix in the heavy cream, butter and milk. Add salt and pepper to taste.

8. Serve with extra butter, salt and pepper.

3,2,1 BLAST OFF RICE PILAF

The Instant Pot® is the perfect rice cooker because it steams it perfectly each and every time. Adding in the veggies makes it extra healthy and extra tasty!

Serves: 8

What You Need:
- 1 tablespoon butter
- 1 small onion, diced
- 1 celery stalk, chopped
- 1/2- 3/4 cup diced carrot
- 2 cups long grain white rice
- 2 cups chicken broth
- 1 cup water
- 1/2 teaspoon salt
- 1 cup frozen peas, thawed
- 2 tablespoons fresh parsley, chopped (optional)
- 1/2 cup sliced almonds or cashews (optional)
- Cooking spray

How You Make It:

1. Spray the inner pot with cooking spray and add the butter. Press the "Sauté" button and allow the butter to melt.

2. Add the carrots, celery and onion to the pot. Cook until the veggies are starting to soften, about 3-4 minutes.

3. Add the uncooked rice and stir it into the veggies and butter. Cook for 1-2 minutes then press the "Keep Warm/Cancel" button.

4. Pour the chicken broth, water and salt into the pot and stir. Place the lid on the pot and close the steam vent.

5. Press the "Manual" button and set the timer for 3 minutes.

6. When the cook time is done, allow the pressure to release naturally for 5 minutes. Then, carefully flip the steam vent to release the remaining pressure.

Veggies and Side Dishes

7 Remove the lid and stir the rice gently. Add the peas, parsley, almonds or cashews if using.

CHEESY VEGETABLE RISOTTO

Risotto is an Italian dish where the rice is cooked in broth until it is tender and creamy. It can be a little hard to make on the stovetop because you have to stir it just the right amount. With the Instant Pot®, you can create perfect risotto with hardly any stirring.

Serves: 6-8

What You Need:
- 1/2 onion, diced into small pieces
- 1 1/2 cups asparagus pieces (trim each stalk of asparagus into 3-4 pieces)
- 3 teaspoons minced garlic
- 2 tablespoons butter
- 2 cups arborio rice
- 3 cups low sodium chicken broth
- 2 tablespoons lemon juice
- 1 teaspoon dried oregano
- 1/2 teaspoon salt
- 1 cup cherry tomatoes or 1 large tomato, diced
- 2/3 cup grated Parmesan cheese
- Cooking spray

How You Make It:

1. Spray the inner pot of the pressure cooker with cooking spray. Press the "Saute" button and add the butter. When the butter has melted, add the onion to the pot. Sauté the onion for about 3 minutes, until it is softened and is just starting to turn light brown.

2. Add the garlic and cook for 1 minute.

3. Add the rice to the pot and stir into the onion and butter. Allow to toast for 2-3 minutes. Press the "Keep Warm/Cancel" button.

4. Pour in the chicken broth, lemon juice, oregano, salt and veggies. Give a quick stir with your spoon or spatula to make sure the rice isn't sticking to the bottom of the pot.

5. Secure the lid and make sure the steam vent is closed. Press the "Manual" button and set the timer for 6 minutes.

6. When the cook time is complete, quick release the pressure and carefully remove the lid.

Veggies and Side Dishes

7 Stir in the Parmesan cheese. When the cheese has fully melted into the risotto, serve big helpings into bowls or onto plates.

PRINCESS AND THE SPLIT PEA SOUP

This is a delicious, hearty soup, that's sure to warm you up on even the coldest day. This is a super easy Instant Pot® soup. Just add all the ingredients to the pot and turn it on. Dinner will be ready soon!

Serves: 8

What You Need:
- 1 pound dried split peas (about 2 1/4 cups)
- 8 cups chicken broth
- 2 cups diced ham chunks
- 1 medium yellow onion, diced
- 1 1/2 cups diced carrots
- 2 stalks celery, diced
- 2 bay leaves
- 2 sprigs fresh thyme

How You Make It:

1. Add all the ingredients to the pot and stir gently. Secure the lid and lock the steam vent into the sealed position.

2. Press the "Soup" button and set the timer for 30 minutes.

3. When the timer beeps after 30 minutes, allow the pressure to release naturally for 10-15 minutes. Then open the steam vent to release any remaining pressure. Carefully open the lid.

4. Stir the soup. Remove the bay leaves and the thyme sprigs. Season with salt and pepper, if needed.

5. Use a ladle to scoop the soup into individual serving bowls and gobble it up!

Veggies and Side Dishes

CHICKEN CORN CHOWDER

The corn and the bacon make this a sweet and savory soup that most kids love. Perfect in the summer when the corn is plentiful or in the winter when you need a good warm meal.

Serves: 6-8

What You Need:
- 6 slices of bacon, plus more if you want some for a topping
- 3 teaspoons minced garlic
- 1 onion, diced
- 1 pound boneless, skinless chicken breasts
- 4 red potatoes, diced
- 1 small carrot, diced
- 1 (16 ounce) package frozen whole kernel corn
- 4 cups chicken stock
- 1 teaspoon dried thyme
- pinch of cayenne pepper (more if you like things spicy)
- 3/4 cup of heavy whipping cream
- 3 tablespoons flour

Tools:
- Tongs
- Whisk
- Mixing Bowl

How You Make It:

1. Press the "Sauté" button on your Instant Pot® and add the bacon to the pot. Cook until bacon is crispy, about 6-8 minutes. Make sure to flip the bacon about halfway through cooking.

2. Use tongs to remove the bacon and place on a paper towel lined plate to drain the grease. When it has cooled, break it into small crumbly pieces.

3. Drain most of the grease from the Instant Pot®, only reserving about 2 teaspoons in the pot. Still using the "Sauté" mode, add the onions and garlic to the pot and cook for about 3 minutes until the onion starts to soften. Press the "Keep Warm/Cancel" button.

4. Add the crumbled bacon, potatoes, carrot, corn, chicken breasts, chicken stock, thyme and a pinch of cayenne pepper. Stir gently and secure the lid. Make sure the steam vent is closed.

Lunch

5. Press the "Manual" button and set the cooking time to 10 minutes.

6. While the soup is cooking use a whisk and a medium mixing bowl to stir together the whipping cream and the flour. Whisk so there are no lumps.

7. When the timer beeps after 10 minutes, open the steam vent and quick release the pressure. Remove the lid.

8. Stir the ingredients and use two forks to shred the chicken that is in the pot.

9. Press the "Sauté" button and bring the soup to a simmer. Add in the whipping cream mixture and stir gently. Allow to cook for an additional 5 minutes, until soup has thickened. If it becomes too thick you can add a little more chicken stock to thin it out.

10. Scoop into bowls and top with shredded cheese and more crumbled bacon if desired.

CREAMY DREAMY TOMATO SOUP

A favorite around our house is a big bowl of creamy tomato soup with a grilled cheese sandwich on the side for dipping.

Serves: 6-8

What You Need:
- 1 medium onion, diced
- 4 tablespoons butter
- 2 (14.5 ounce) cans diced tomatoes
- 1 (46 ounce) bottle of tomato juice
- 3-6 tablespoons sugar
- 3 chicken bouillon cubes
- 1/2 teaspoon ground black pepper
- 1 1/2 cups heavy whipping cream

How You Make It:

1. Press the "Sauté" button on the Instant Pot® and add the butter to the pot. When the butter has melted, dump the onions into the butter and stir gently. Cook until the onions are beginning to soften, about 3-4 minutes.

2. Press the "Keep Warm/ Cancel" button.

3. Pour in the diced tomatoes and tomato juice. Add 3 tablespoons of sugar and check to see if it is sweet enough. If it needs more sugar, continue adding, one tablespoon at a time until desired taste is reached.

4. Stir in the chicken bouillon cubes and the pepper. Secure the lid and make sure the steam vent is sealed.

5. Press the "Manual" button and set the timer for 10 minutes.

6. When the cook time is complete, allow the pressure to reduce naturally for 10 minutes before opening the steam vent to release the remaining pressure.

7. Remove the lid and pour the heavy cream into the pot. Stir gently.

Lunch

Tip for Success

Tomatoes are a pretty acidic food that can have a powerful taste. The sugar helps to lightly sweeten the tomatoes, which enhances their flavor. Some tomatoes tend to be more acidic than others, so always taste your soup as you are making it. Add about three tablespoons then taste to see how much more you need to add to make it just right for you.

8 Serve with a side of crusty bread or better yet, a grilled cheese sandwich!

CHICKEN SALAD SANDWICHES

Using the Instant Pot® to prepare the chicken for chicken salad sandwiches is a game changer. It makes preparing chicken salad so much easier. Experiment with substituting your favorite fruits and nuts in the salad. Try cranberries, cashews or even pineapple!

Serves: makes 4-6 sandwiches

What You Need:
- 1 pound boneless, skinless, chicken breasts
- 2/3 cup apple, peeled, core removed and diced
- 2/3 cup grapes, sliced in half
- 1/4 cup sliced almonds
- 1/2–2/3 cup mayonnaise
- 1 teaspoon lemon zest
- 1 tablespoon lemon juice
- 1/4 teaspoon garlic powder
- Bread, buns or rolls of your choice to make the sandwiches

Tools:
- Tongs
- Large Mixing Bowl

Tongs

How You Make It:

1. Add 1 cup of water to the inner pot of the pressure cooker. Add the chicken into the pot.

2. Close the lid and make sure the steam vent is sealed. Press the "Manual" button and set the timer for 10 minutes.

3. When the timer beeps, open up the steam vent to release the pressure. Use tongs to remove the chicken from the pot and place on a large plate. Set aside to cool.

4. When the chicken has cooled, use two forks to shred the chicken into very small pieces.

5. Place the chicken in a large mixing bowl and add in the other ingredients. Mix until they are all well combined.

6. If you are serving right away, scoop the chicken salad onto the bread or rolls of your choice. If not, place it in a container with a lid and store in the refrigerator.

Lunch

Tasty Tip
Start with only a 1/2 cup of mayonnaise and add more if you like your chicken salad with a little more "sauce." Keep mixing until your desired consistency is reached.

Tip for Success
For the lemon zest, use a fine grater or a zestor to grate or rub the outside skin of the lemon peel.

BAKED POTATO HEADS

Baked potatoes are a great lunch. They are filling, healthy and can be topped with your favorite ingredients to make them super tasty!

Serves: makes 2 potatoes

What You Need:
- 2 medium sized potatoes
- 2 cups water (for bottom of the Inner Pot)
- Topping Ideas:
- 4 teaspoon butter
- 6 tablespoons shredded cheddar cheese
- 4 tablespoons sour cream or plain Greek yogurt
- or
- 1/4 cup salsa

Tools:
- Trivet
- Tongs

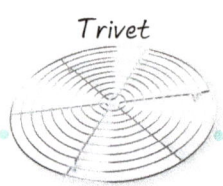

How You Make It:

1. Place 2 cups water into the inner pot of the pressure cooker and set the trivet in the pot.

2. Scrub the potatoes well under running water. Pierce each potato several times with a fork. This will prevent it from breaking open while it is cooking.

3. Place the clean potatoes on the trivet. Secure the lid and close the steam vent.

4. Press the "Manual" button and set the timer for 15 minutes.

5. When the timer beeps after 15 minutes, allow the pressure to release naturally for 10 minutes before opening the steam vent.

6. Use tongs to remove the baked potatoes. Set them on separate plates and allow them to cool for about 5 minutes.

7. Cut the potatoes open, being careful because they will release a lot of steam.

8. Top the potatoes with your favorite toppings. Some good ideas are butter, cheese and sour cream or your favorite salsa.

Lunch

Tasty Tip

I listed a few of our favorite potato toppings, but get creative. Try chili, nacho cheese sauce, broccoli or even taco meat on your potato. The possibilities are endless!

Tip for Success

Big potatoes may take longer to cook. Fifteen minutes should be plenty of time for medium potatoes, but try 20 or even 25 minutes if your potatoes are large. You can cook up to 8 medium sized potatoes without increasing the cook time, so you can cook them for a crowd of friends!

MACARONI AND CHEESE, PLEASE!

Cheesy macaroni noodles are always a kid pleaser, but its extra fun when you make them yourself.

Serves: 4

What You Need:
- 8 ounces uncooked elbow macaroni
- 2 cups low sodium chicken broth
- 1 tablespoon butter
- 1/2 teaspoon salt
- 1/4 teaspoon garlic powder
- 1/4 teaspoon pepper
- 1 cup shredded cheddar cheese
- 1/4 cup shredded mozzarella
- 1/2 cup milk
- Cooking Spray

How You Make It:

1. Spray the inside pot of your pressure cooker with cooking spray. Add to the pot the chicken broth, macaroni, butter, salt, pepper and garlic powder. Give a quick stir to the ingredients.

2. Secure the lid and close the steam vent. Press the "Manual" button and set the timer for 5 minutes.

3. When the timer beeps, allow the pressure to release naturally for 10 minutes. then open the steam vent to release any remaining pressure.

4. Stir the noodles and add in the cheese. Use an oven bit to hold the pot while you stir as the noodles will be thick. Add the milk until the mixture becomes creamy.

5. Make sure all the cheese has melted and serve yourself a heaping bowl!

Lunch

Tasty Tip
You can use 2 1/2 cups of whatever cheese you like. Or mix and match. You want to mostly use a cheese that will melt well like cheddar, gruyere, or Monterey jack. Mix in a little of the other cheeses like Parmesan, mozzarella or provolone. Experiment with what you have on hand until you find your perfect blend!

STEP RIGHT UP, GET YER HOT DOGS!

If you've had the pleasure of eating a hot dog from a street vendor you know that they are so full of flavor. Here, we use some seasonings you probably have in your parents' spice rack to create similar flavors. Make sure you use the good hot dogs with casings, not the skinless kind.

Serves: makes 4-8 hot dogs

What You Need:
- 4-8 hot dogs with casings
- 4 cups water
- 1 tablespoon white vinegar
- 1/2 teaspoon ground cumin
- 1/8 teaspoon ground nutmeg

Tools:
- Tongs

Tongs

How You Make It:

1. Pour the water into the inner pot and stir in the vinegar, cumin and nutmeg.

2. Add the hotdogs, being sure they are covered in the water.

3. Close the lid and make sure the steam vent is in the sealed position.

Lunch

4. Press the "Manual" button then press the "Pressure" button to adjust to low pressure. Set the timer for 3 minutes.

5. When the timer beeps after 3 minutes, quick release the pressure. Watch out for the steam!

6. Use tongs to remove the hot dogs. Serve them with buns and your favorite toppings.

CHICKEN TACOS (DRAGON APPROVED)

Everybody loves tacos! Whether you serve soft shell or corn tortillas, these chicken tacos are super easy to make and sure to be a hit with your friends, family, or any dragons you know. (They love tacos.)

Serves: 4

What You Need:
- 3 boneless, skinless chicken breasts
- 2 tablespoons of taco seasoning (either pre-packaged or homemade)
- 1 cup tomato salsa
- 1/3 cup chicken broth
- Cooking Spray

How You Make It:

1 Spray the inner pot of the pressure cooker with cooking spray to make clean-up easier.

2 Pour the chicken broth into the pot. Add the chicken breasts to the bottom.

3 Sprinkle the taco seasonings onto the chicken. Top with the salsa.

4 Secure the lid and close the steam vent.

5 Press the "Manual" button and set the timer for 10 minutes.

6 When the timer beeps after 10 minutes, quick release the pressure.

7 Open the lid and use two forks to shred the chicken breasts. Mix well with the sauce and serve with taco shells, cheese and your other favorite taco toppings.

Dinner - Poultry

Tip for Success

If you like beans and corn and want to make your tacos even more filling and flavorful, add 1 cup of frozen corn and 1(15 ounce) can of black beans that have been drained and rinsed to the chicken when you pour in the salsa. The cooking time will be the same, but you will have more tasty flavor.

CHEESY STUFFED CHICKEN IN ALFREDO SAUCE

Simply dumping out a jar of Alfredo sauce to cook the chicken in along with a bit of seasoning makes for tender, cheesy chicken and the most delicious sauce. I've kept this one simple, but when it's on the plate…it looks really fancy.

Serves: 4

What You Need:
- 4 boneless, skinless chicken breasts, pounded thin
- 1 cup of shredded cheddar cheese
- 1 (15 ounce) jar Alfredo sauce
- 1 teaspoon mixed Italian herbs
- 1/8 teaspoon salt
- 1/8 teaspoon ground black pepper
- 2 teaspoons olive oil

Tools:
- Cooking Spray
- Wax Paper
- Wooden Cooking Mallet or Rolling Pin
- Toothpicks

How You Make It:

1 Lay your chicken on a cutting board and cover with a large piece of wax paper. Use a wooden cooking mallet (you can also use a wooden rolling pin if you don't have the mallet) to pound the chicken. You want it to all be about the same thickness when done, about 1/2 inch thick. So don't go crazy.

2 Divide the Italian herbs, salt and pepper amongst the chicken breasts and sprinkle onto each breast. Make sure to get some on both sides of the chicken. Scoop 2 tablespoons of shredded cheese onto each breast.

3 Roll each chicken breast so the cheese is in the middle and secure with a toothpick.

4 Spray the inner pot of your Instant Pot® with cooking spray. Add the olive oil and press the "Sauté" button.

5 When the oil is hot, add the chicken and brown lightly on the bottom. Carefully flip it over and lightly brown the other side. When both sides are slightly golden, press the "Keep Warm/ Cancel" button on your Instant Pot®.

Dinner - Poultry

Tasty Tip

Don't let all that yummy sauce go to waste! Pour it over your green veggies to give them a little pizzaz. Broccoli and spinach are delicious with this sauce.

6 Pour in the Alfredo sauce, being sure to coat all the chicken.

7 Secure the lid and be sure the steam valve is closed.

8 Press the "Manual" button and set the timer for 10 minutes.

9 When the timer beeps, flip the steam vent to open to release the pressure.

10 Carefully remove the chicken breasts. Place on serving plates and then spoon some of the Alfredo sauce onto the top. Sprinkle the top of the chicken with any remaining shredded cheese.

SWEET AND SASSY HONEY CHICKEN

This chicken is cooked in a sauce that reminds me a little of my favorite Chinese food. It's sweet and savory at the same time. I like to serve it over rice to soak up some of the additional sauce.

Serves: 2-3

What You Need:
- 1/4 cup chicken stock
- 1/4 cup reduced sodium soy sauce
- 1/4 cup honey
- 1 tablespoon sesame oil
- 1/8 teaspoon red pepper flakes (optional, if you like it a little spicy)
- 2 large chicken breasts, thawed
- 1 tablespoon cornstarch
- 2 tablespoons water
- Cooking Spray

How You Make It:

1. Spray the inner pot of the pressure cooker with cooking spray.

2. Cut the chicken breast into 2-3 pieces, equal in size.

3. In the inner pot, mix together the chicken stock, honey, soy sauce, sesame oil and red pepper flakes. Stir until it's all nice and evenly mixed.

4. Add the chicken and coat in the sauce.

5. Close the lid and be sure the steam vent is in the closed position.

6. Press the "Manual" button and set the timer for 8 minutes.

7. When the timer beeps after 8 minutes, open the steam vent to release the pressure.

8. Remove the chicken breasts and set on a plate while you finish the sauce.

Dinner - Poultry

9 Stir together the cornstarch and water until completely mixed. Add to the sauce in the pot and stir well.

10 Press the "Sauté" button and allow the sauce to come to a simmer, stirring frequently. When the sauce has thickened, press the "Keep Warm/Cancel" button.

11 Add the chicken back to the pot and stir to cover in the sauce. the "Keep Warm/Cancel" button.

12 Serve the chicken breasts topped with additional sauce. ened, press the "Keep Warm/Cancel" button.

ROSEMARY LEMON "BIG OLE" WHOLE CHICKEN

Cooking a WHOLE chicken looks so impressive…and difficult. But it's actually very easy if you are using the Instant Pot®. The hardest part will be dealing with the size of the chicken- they are heavy and a little awkward. So ask a grownup for some help and your whole house can enjoy this tasty dinner.

Serves: 4-6

What You Need:
- 4 pound whole chicken
- 1 1/2 teaspoons salt
- 1/2 teaspoon ground black pepper
- 1 teaspoon garlic powder
- 1 teaspoon paprika
- 1 teaspoon dried rosemary
- 2 teaspoons canola oil
- 1 yellow onion, cut into four pieces
- 1 lemon, cut in half
- 4 lemon slices
- 2 sprigs of fresh rosemary
- 1 cup chicken stock

How You Make It:

1 Remove chicken giblets from the cavity (thats the inside) of the chicken. Rinse the chicken in the sink and use some paper towels to pat it dry.

2 Stuff the inner cavity with the onion, 1 lemon cut in half and the rosemary sprigs.

3 In a small bowl mix together the salt, pepper, garlic powder, rosemary and paprika. Add the oil and mix well.

4 Press the "Sauté" button on the Instant Pot® to begin to warm the pot.

5 Use your fingers to rub the oil and spice mixture all over the bird, including under the wings and inside the cavity.

6 Place the chicken with the breast side down inside the Instant Pot®. Allow it to brown for 3-4 minutes.

Dinner - Poultry

7 Use tongs or a spatula to flip the chicken to the other side and allow to brown again for 3-4 minutes. You may need to ask an adult for help.

8 Pour the chicken stock into the pot. Top the chicken with the 4 lemon slices. Close the lid and be sure the pressure valve is closed.

9 Press the "Manual" button and set the timer for 25 minutes.

10 When the timer beeps after 25 minutes, allow the pressure to release naturally. Do not flip open the pressure valve. (This will take about 15 minutes.)

11 When the silver floating valve drops down, you can open the lid. Use tongs to remove the chicken from the pot and place it on a serving platter.

Tip for Success

The chicken will be very tender, so have a grown up help you transfer the chicken to the serving platter. When it's time to eat, spoon some of the cooking juices in the bottom of the pot over the top of the chicken. Place the lemon slices on top of the chicken for added garnish.

PINEAPPLE CHICKEN "THAT'S JUST MAUI MESSIN' AROUND"

Our family loves cooking up this sweet dish. Pineapples aren't just for Hawaiian luau's! Be sure to use a barbecue sauce that isn't too spicy or the sauce could end up being a bit spicy.

Serves: 4-6

What You Need:
- 1 1/2 pounds boneless, skinless chicken breasts
- 1 (20 ounce) can of pineapple chunks with juice
- 1 (18 ounce) bottle honey barbecue sauce
- 1 1/2 tablespoons cornstarch
- 1 1/2 tablespoons water

Tools:
- Cooking Spray
- Ladle

Ladle

How You Make It:

1 Spray the inner pot with cooking spray. Add the chicken breasts, pineapple chunks and juice and the barbecue sauce to the pot.

2 Close the lid and make sure the steam vent is closed.

3 Press the "Manual" button and adjust the cook time to 12 minutes.

4 When the timer beeps, open the steam vent to release the pressure. Watch out for the steam!

5 Use a ladle to scoop out the chicken and pineapple chunks, but leave the sauce in the pot. Place the chicken and pineapple in a large serving bowl and shred the chicken into smaller pieces. The easiest way to do this is to use two forks.

6 Press the "Sauté" button on the Instant Pot®.

Dinner - Poultry

7 Mix together the cornstarch and water until the cornstarch has dissolved completely. Add it to the pot and stir until it's mixed in with the sauce.

8 Simmer 1-2 minutes to thicken the sauce. Turn off the Instant Pot® and pour the sauce over the chicken. Stir to combine and serve.

Tasty Tip

This meal tastes kind of like sweet and sour chicken and is easy to make. It tastes delicious served over rice with a side vegetables.

BBQ CHICKEN SLIDERS

Safe at home plate! These chicken sliders are super easy to make and even easier to eat. This recipe will double if you are feeding a crowd.

Serves: makes 6 sliders

What You Need:
- 1 pound boneless, skinless chicken breasts
- 3/4 cup of barbecue sauce
- 1/2 cup low sodium chicken broth
- 1 tablespoon Worcestershire Sauce
- 1 teaspoon unsweetened cocoa powder
- 1/4 teaspoon salt
- 1/4 teaspoon pepper
- 6 Hawaiian sweet rolls or slider buns

How You Make It:

1 Lightly spray the inner pot with cooking spray.

2 Season the chicken by sprinkling it with the salt, pepper and cocoa powder.

3 Pour the chicken broth and Worcestershire into the pot. Add the seasoned chicken. Top with the barbecue sauce.

4 Close the lid and be sure the steam valve is sealed. Press the "Manual" button and set the timer for 10 minutes.

5 When the timer beeps after 10 minutes, open the steam valve to release the pressure. Carefully open the lid.

6 Remove the chicken breasts to a large platter or bowl and use two forks to shred the meat.

7 Place the shredded meat back into the pot ad mix in the sauce.

8 Scoop the BBQ chicken onto the buns and serve with additional BBQ sauce on the side. Top with creamy coleslaw if you'd like.

Dinner - Poultry

PRESTO PESTO CHICKEN PACKETS

What a fun and healthy meal to make for yourself! Cooking the chicken in the foil packet makes for easy clean-up. Toss with pasta and extra pesto for a complete meal.

Serves: 1

What You Need:
- 1 boneless, skinless chicken breast
- 2 tablespoons of pesto
- 1/4 cup grape tomatoes
- Pinch salt
- Pinch pepper
- 1-2 tablespoons grated Parmesan cheese

Tools:
- 1 Piece Tinfoil 12 Inches Long
- Trivet
- Tongs
- Cooking Spray

How You Make It:

1 Season a chicken breast with a pinch of salt and pepper.

2 Cut the chicken breast into small cubes about 1 inch in size. Place them in a bowl and add the pesto. Mix well so all the cubes of chicken are coated in the pesto.

3 Spray one side of a piece of tinfoil with cooking spray. Pour the pesto chicken cubes into the middle of the tinfoil.

4 Add the grape tomatoes to the top of the chicken.

5 Fold all sides of the tinfoil inward creating a sealed packet for the chicken.

6 Pour 2 cups of water into the inner pot of the Instant Pot®. Place the trivet in the pot.

7 Place the sealed packet on top of the trivet and close the lid. Be sure the steam vent is in the closed position.

8 Press the "Manual" button and set the timer for 12 minutes.

Dinner - Poultry

9 When the timer beeps after 12 minutes, open the steam vent and release the pressure.

10 Using tongs, carefully remove the packet and place on a plate. Open the packets and use a spoon to scoop the chicken and tomatoes to a plate.

11 Top the chicken and tomatoes with Parmesan cheese. Enjoy!

Tasty Tip

You can make individual packets for your family and friends and cook them in the pressure cooker all at the same time!

CHICKEN NOODLE "SICK DAY" SOUP

Chicken noodle soup is yummy anytime, but especially if you or someone you care about is sick. Show someone you care by trying out this new and delicious recipe.

Serves: 4

What You Need:
- 1 tablespoon butter
- 1 small onion, diced
- 3/4 cup diced carrots
- 1 teaspoon minced garlic
- 1 celery stalk, diced
- 1/2 teaspoon salt
- 1/2 teaspoon ground black pepper
- 1/2 teaspoon dried thyme
- 1 teaspoon dried parsley
- 1 teaspoon dried oregano
- 1 bay leaf
- 2 cups chicken broth, low sodium
- 2 cups water
- 1 pound chicken breasts, with bones and skin
- 1 1/2 cups dried egg noodles

How You Make It:

1 Press the "Sauté" button on your Instant Pot® and add the butter to the pot. When the butter has melted add the onion, celery and carrot to the pot and cook until they begin to soften, about 3-4 minutes. Add the garlic and cook for one more minute.

2 Pour 2 cups of chicken broth and 2 cups of water into the pot and season with salt, pepper, thyme, parsley, oregano and the bay leaf. Stir gently. Press the "Keep Warm/Cancel" button.

3 Place the chicken into the pot. Close the lid and make sure the steam valve is in the sealed position.

Dinner - Poultry

4 Press the "Soup" button and set the timer for 7 minutes.

5 When the cooking cycle is complete and the timer beeps, allow the pressure to release naturally for 10 minutes. Then you can flip the steam vent open and release the pressure.

6 Use a large slotted spoon to remove the chicken pieces from the pot and place on a plate. Remove the bay leaf and discard.

7 Add the dried egg noddles to the pot and press the "Sauté" button. Cook the noodles in the pot for 6 minutes.

8 While the noodles are cooking, remove the chicken meat from the bones. Discard the skin and bones and shred the meat into small pieces.

9 When the noodles are done cooking, add the chicken meat into the pot. Stir the soup gently and serve.

SLOPPY JOE, SLOP SLOPPY JOE

This sloppy joe recipe has a few secret ingredients… healthy vegetables! But don't worry, you won't even know they are there. Ground beef cooked in a savory sauce makes for a delicious meal your whole family will love.

Serves: 6

What You Need:
- 1 1/2 pounds lean ground beef
- 1 teaspoon olive oil
- 1/2 large onion, diced
- 1 red bell pepper, diced (about 1/2 cup)
- 5-6 tablespoons grated carrots (optional)
- 2 teaspoons minced garlic
- 1/2 cup beef broth
- 1/2 cup ketchup
- 2 teaspoons brown sugar
- 1 tablespoon tomato paste
- 2 tablespoons yellow mustard
- 1 tablespoon apple cider vinegar
- 2 tablespoons Worcestershire sauce
- 1/2 tablespoon chili powder
- 1 tablespoon cornstarch
- 1-2 tablespoons water

Tools:
- Grater, if using carrots
- Cooking Spray

How You Make It:

1 Prepare all of your ingredients by dicing all your vegetables and grating the carrots if you are using them.

2 In a medium sized mixing bowl, stir together the ketchup, beef broth, brown sugar, tomato paste, mustard, vinegar, Worcestershire sauce and the chili powder until well mixed.

3 Spray the inner pot with cooking spray. Press the "Sauté" button and add 1 teaspoon olive oil. Add you ground beef and the onions, peppers and carrots. Cook until the beef is browned, chopping it up as you go. In the last 2 minutes, add the garlic. Press the "Keep Warm/Cancel" button when the cooking is done.

4 Use a colander to drain any excess grease from the meat and vegetables.

Dinner - Beef

5 Add the meat and vegetables back to the pot. Pour the red sauce on top and stir gently.

6 Close the lid and make sure the steam valve is turned to the sealed position.

7 Press the "Manual" button and adjust your timer to 7 minutes.

8 While the sloppy joe's are cooking, mix together the cornstarch and water. You want to add just enough water so that the cornstarch dissolves. This will help thicken the sloppy joe's when they are done cooking.

9 When the cooking time is complete, carefully flip the steam valve open to quick release the pressure.

10 Press the "Sauté" button and stir the cornstarch and water mixture into the pot. Stir well and allow the meat to come to a simmer, while stirring frequently. Simmer until some of the liquid has evaporated and sloppy joe's are a little less sloppy. You get to pick how sloppy you like them!

11 Serve the meat on toasted buns.

Tasty Tip

For a fun and healthy variation, try serving the sloppy Joe meat over salad or even a baked potato.

WILLY NILLY CHILI

Chili is very simple to make and is easy to adapt to your own tastes simply by adjusting the seasonings. This recipe will give you a great base for flavorful, but not too spicy chili. Then you can adjust the seasonings to create your signature dish. Who knows? Maybe you can win a chili cook-off one day!

Serves: 6-8

What You Need:
- 1 1/2 pounds lean ground beef
- 1 small onion diced (if you like onion)
- 1 1/2 cups beef broth
- 2 (15 ounce) cans mild chili beans
- 1 (15 ounce) can red kidney beans
- 1 cup diced tomatoes with juices
- 1 (8 ounce) can tomato sauce
- 1-2 tablespoons chili powder (depending on how spicy you like your chili)
- 1 tablespoon ground cumin
- 1 teaspoon garlic powder
- 1 teaspoon oregano
- 1/2 teaspoon salt
- 1 tablespoon tomato paste

How You Make It:

1 Spray your inner pot lightly with cooking spray. Press the "Sauté" button on your Instant Pot® and add the ground beef and onion to the pot. Cook until all the meat is browned, chopping it apart as it cooks. If you aren't using lean ground beef you may need to drain the grease before adding the rest of the ingredients.

2 Pour in the beef broth and scrape at the bottom of the pot to release any browned bits. This is called 'deglazing' the pot. The browned bits add great flavor to whatever you are cooking.

3 Add the rest of the ingredients and stir gently.

4 Apply the lid and secure it tightly. Make sure the steam valve is closed.

Dinner - Beef

Tip for Success

If you need to remove grease from the cooked ground beef, gather a large mixing bowl and a colander. Place the colander so that it sits inside the mixing bowl. Pour the cooked ground meat into the colander. The colander will allow the grease to drain from the meat into the mixing bowl. After the grease has drained, transfer the meat back to the inner pot. Pour the grease into a steel can and allow it to harden in the freezer before throwing into the trash. You don't want to pour the grease down the sink as it could clog it up.

5 Press the "Manual" button and set the timer for 12 minutes.

6 When the timer beeps after 12 minutes, let the pressure release naturally for 15 minutes. Then you can flip the steam vent to open position to release any remaining pressure.

7 Open the lid carefully and stir the chili.

8 Use a ladle to scoop the chili into bowls and serve with shredded cheese, corn chips, diced onion or avocado.

"KNOCK YOUR SOCKS OFF" BEEF STROGANOFF

This is a hearty meal, meant for cold nights. It was originally a Russian dish, but now variations are served worldwide. The creamy sauce and tender beef served over noodles is definitely a kid pleaser.

Serves: 4-6

What You Need:
- 2 pounds of beef stewing meat
- 1 teaspoon salt
- 1/2 teaspoon ground black pepper
- 1/2 teaspoon dried parsley
- 1/2 teaspoon onion powder
- 1 tablespoon olive oil
- 3 tablespoons butter
- 1 tablespoon minced garlic
- 8 ounces sliced fresh mushrooms
- 1 onion, diced
- 1 1/2 cups beef broth
- 2 tablespoons flour
- 2 tablespoons Worcestershire sauce
- 1/2 cup sour cream
- 12 ounces egg noodles, cooked, for serving

How You Make It:

1 Mix together the salt, pepper, parsley and onion powder and sprinkle it all over the beef cubes, coating all sides.

2 Pour the olive oil into the inner pot of the pressure cooker and press the "Sauté" button. After about 3 minutes, when the oil is hot, add the beef to the pot and begin to brown. Cook until brown on all sides, about 5-6 minutes, stirring regularly to promote even cooking. It's okay if some of the pieces get a dark brown coating. This adds great flavor!

3 When the meat is browned, use a spatula to place the meat on a plate. Add the butter to the inner pot and allow it to melt. Put the onions and mushrooms into the pot and cook in the butter until soft, about 3-4 minutes.

4 Add the minced garlic and cook for one more minute. Press the "Keep Warm/Cancel" button.

Dinner - Beef

5 Pour in 1/2 cup beef broth and scrape at the bottom of the pot to release any of the browned bits. This is called deglazing the pot. The browned bits really add flavor!

6 Place the meat back in the pot and add the rest of the beef broth and the Worcestershire sauce. Secure the lid and close the steam vent.

7 Press the "Manual" button and set the timer for 13 minutes.

8 When the timer beeps, allow the pressure to release naturally for 10 minutes. Then, carefully flip the steam vent and release any remaining pressure.

9 Open the lid and press the "Sauté" button.

10 Mix together the sour cream and the flour and add to the pot. Stir to fully dissolve the sour cream into the sauce.

11 Cook for several minutes while the sauce thickens. Turn off the pot and serve the beef stroganoff over egg noddles for a delicious feast!

SPAGHETTI

I think most of us will agree that spaghetti is one delicious meal. Noodles mixed with flavorful tomato sauce, topped with a little cheese makes for a fun and tasty dinnertime. Try saying it like a cartoon Italian chef, "Spa-gaaaaaytti".

Serves: 6

What You Need:
- 1 pound ground beef, lean ground beef preferred
- 2 teaspoons minced garlic
- 12 ounces dry spaghetti noodles
- 1 (24 ounce) jar spaghetti sauce
- 1 (14.5 ounce) can diced tomatoes
- 2 2/3 cups warm water
- Parmesan cheese, shredded or grated, for serving
- Cooking spray

How You Make It:

1 Spray the inner pot with cooking spray. Press the "Sauté" button on the Instant Pot®. Add the ground beef to the pot and cook until browned, chopping it into small pieces as it cooks.

2 Drain any grease from the meat and then place it back into the pot. Add the garlic and continue to cook for 1-2 more minutes. Press the "Keep Warm/Cancel" button.

3 To add the spaghetti noodles, break the dry noodles in half. Layer some of the noodles going one direction and then other noodles going the opposite direction. Do this about 3 times. This just helps so the noodles won't stick together so much.

Dinner - Beef

4 Add in the spaghetti sauce, diced tomatoes and water to the top of the noodles. Do not stir, but be sure the noodles are all covered with the sauce.

5 Secure the lid and be sure the steam vent is closed. Press the "Manual" button and set the cook time for 7 minutes.

6 When the cook time is complete, open the steam vent to release the pressure. Carefully remove the lid.

7 Stir the spaghetti to fully mix the noodles, meat and sauce. Allow the pasta to sit for about 2 minutes before serving. This will help the pasta absorb more of the sauce.

8 Scoop the spaghetti onto plates and top with Parmesan cheese.

MAGNIFICENT MEATLOAF MUFFINS

Not only do these meatloaf muffins look cute and taste great, they are a great option to make ahead to have on hand for lunch or snacks. You can stick what you don't eat in the refrigerator or freezer to eat later.

Serves: 6

What You Need:
Meatloaf:
- 1 pound lean ground beef
- 1/2 cup quick cook oats
- 1/2 cup ketchup
- 1 tablespoon Worcestershire
- 1 egg

Sauce: (optional)
- 1/3 cup ketchup
- 2 tablespoons mustard
- 2 tablespoons brown sugar

Tools:
- Silicone Muffin Cups
- Trivet
- Tongs

How You Make It:

1 In a large bowl, add the beef, oats, ketchup, Worcestershire and the egg. Use your clean hands or a mixer to blend the ingredients until they are well combined. Be prepared, it will be cold on your hands! So feel free to take a break and warm them at the sink by rinsing in warm water if you need to and then dive back in.

2 Form the meat mixture into little balls, about 3 inches in size. Place each mini meatloaf into one of the silicone muffin cups.

3 If you are going to use the sauce for topping the meatloaf muffins, mix the ingredients together in a small bowl. Use a spoon to drizzle the sauce onto the top of each mini meatloaf. Save any leftovers for dipping.

Dinner - Beef

4 Pour 1 cup of water into the bottom of the inner pot of the pressure cooker. Place the trivet into the pot. Put the muffin cups with the mini meatloaves onto the top of the trivet. You can use a second trivet to add another layer of muffin cups, or you can cook in batches. This recipe makes 6-8 mini meatloaf muffins, depending on how big you make them.

5 Secure the lid and close the steam vent. Press the "Manual" button and set the timer for 30 minutes.

6 When the timer beeps after 30 minutes, open the steam vent to release the pressure. Carefully open the lid.

7 Use tongs or an oven mitt to reach into the pot and remove the meatloaf muffins.

8 Use tongs or a fork to transfer the mini meatloaf muffins to a plate and serve with any additional sauce or ketchup on the side.

BIG KID BEEF AND BROCCOLI

Beef and broccoli is usually a Chinese food takeout favorite. Did you know it's much healthier to make your own version at home? This recipe is so tasty you won't even miss the takeout variety. Serve over rice to help soak up some of the delicious sauce.

Serves: 4

What You Need:
- 1 1/2 pounds boneless chuck roast beef, sliced into thin strips
- 1 (12 ounce) steamer bag of frozen broccoli (to microwave)
- 4 teaspoons minced garlic
- 1 tablespoon canola oil
- 1/2 cup beef broth
- 1/2 cup low-sodium soy sauce
- 1/4 cup brown sugar
- 1 tablespoon corn starch
- 1 tablespoon water

How You Make It:

1 Press the "Sauté" button on your Instant Pot® and add the canola oil to the inner pot. When the oil is hot, add the beef.

2 Cook the beef until browned lightly on all sides, stirring several times to flip the meat. Add the garlic to the pot and cook for one more minute.

3 Pour in the beef broth, soy sauce and brown sugar. Stir to dissolve the sugar. Press the "Keep Warm/Cancel" button.

4 Close the lid and be sure the steam vent is in the sealed position. Select the "Manual" button and set the timer for 15 minutes.

5 While the beef is cooking in the Instant Pot®, follow the directions on your steamer bag of broccoli and cook it in the microwave.

6 When the beef has completed cooking, quick release the pressure by carefully opening the steam vent.

Dinner - Beef

7 Mix together 1 tablespoon of water and 1 tablespoon of cornstarch in a small bowl. Add this mixture to the pot and stir to thicken the sauce. This will take about 5 minutes.

8 Add the broccoli to the pot and stir to coat in the sauce. It's delicious served over rice.

COUNTRY STYLE BONELESS PORK RIBS

Boneless pork ribs are perfect for the Instant Pot® because they become so tender and flavorful when cooked this way. This recipe uses a dry rub to bring a lot of flavor to the meat. The meat is then cooked in barbecue sauce until it is juicy and tender. Yum!

Serves: 4-6

What You Need:
- 2 pounds country style pork ribs (boneless)
- 3 tablespoons brown sugar
- 3 tablespoons paprika
- 1/4 teaspoon onion powder
- 1/2 teaspoon salt
- 1/2 teaspoon ground black pepper
- 1/2 teaspoon garlic powder
- 1/2 cup chicken stock
- 1/2 cup honey barbecue sauce

Tools:
- Cooking Spray
- Tongs

Tongs

How You Make It:

1. In a small bowl mix together the brown sugar, paprika, onion powder, salt, pepper and garlic powder. This will be a dry rub for your pork.

2. Use your clean hands to rub the dry rub all over the pork rib pieces. You want the meat to be well coated in the spices.

3. Spray the liner of the pressure cooker with cooking spray and add 1/2 cup chicken broth. Place the ribs into the pot and top with the barbecue sauce.

4. Secure the lid and close the steam vent. Press the "Manual" button and select a cook time of 22 minutes.

Dinner - Pork

5 When the timer beeps after 22 minutes, allow the pressure to release naturally for at least 10 minutes. Then open the steam vent to release any pressure.

6 Use tongs to remove the chunks of meat and set on a plate or serving platter.

7 Press the "Sauté" button and bring the cooking liquid to a simmer. Simmer for about 5 minutes or until the sauce has thickened a bit.

8 Serve the ribs topped with the sauce and serve with additional barbecue sauce on the side if desired.

PULLED PORK IN BBQ SAUCE

Smoked barbecue meat is delicious but takes a long time and special tools to make. You can make incredible barbecue right in the Instant Pot®. If you can place ingredients into the pot, you can make this pulled pork. Perfect for sandwiches or serve it up on a salad or baked potato.

Serves: 6

What You Need:
- 1 cup ketchup
- 1/2 cup chicken stock
- 1/4 cup honey
- 1/4 cup Worcestershire Sauce
- 2 tablespoons apple cider vinegar
- 1/2 tablespoon paprika
- 1/4 teaspoon cayenne pepper
- 2 teaspoons garlic powder
- 1/2 teaspoon mustard powder
- 1 teaspoon salt
- 2 pounds boneless pork shoulder
- Cooking Spray

How You Make It:

1 In a medium mixing bowl, stir together the ketchup, chicken stock, honey, Worcestershire sauce, apple cider vinegar, paprika, cayenne, garlic powder, mustard powder and salt. Mix it up really good.

2 Spray the inner pot of the pressure cooker with the cooking spray. Pour half of the sauce mixture into the pot.

3 Place the pork into the pot. Pour the remaining sauce on top of the pork.

4 Close the lid and be sure the steam vent is sealed.

5 Press the "Manual" button and set the timer for 90 minutes.

6 Allow the pressure to release naturally for 15 minutes when the timer beeps. Then open the steam valve and release any remaining pressure.

Dinner - Pork

Tip for Success

Transfer the meat to a large plate or platter to shred. Its usually easiest to work in 2 or 3 batches, so you aren't trying to shred the whole chunk of meat at once. Use two forks and just pull at the meat until the pieces are as small as you want them. It will be tender, so it won't be hard to pull apart.

7 Use two forks to shred the meat. Stir the meat into the sauce at the bottom of the pot.

8 Serve just as it is or add it to your favorite bun or bread.

PORK TENDERLOIN IN BALSAMIC APPLE SAUCE

Do you have a favorite season of the year? I love fall or autumn and this recipe tastes like fall on a plate. It's a bit of an involved recipe with some peeling and chopping, so ask a grown-up for some help and enjoy spending time creating this delicious dish together.

Serves: 4

What You Need:
- 1 tablespoon olive oil
- 1 1/2 pounds pork tenderloin
- 2 teaspoons minced garlic
- 2 1/2 tablespoons balsamic vinegar
- 1/2 cup apple juice
- 2-3 apples, peeled, cored and diced into 1 inch chunks
- 1/2 teaspoon salt
- 1 teaspoon dried thyme
- 1/2 teaspoon dried rosemary
- 2 tablespoons honey
- 1 tablespoon butter
- 1 tablespoon cornstarch
- 1 tablespoon water

Tools:
- Tongs or Spatula

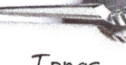
Tongs

How You Make It:

1 Peel and core the apple then cut it into 1 inch chunks.

2 Pour olive oil into the inner pot and press the "Sauté" button. After about 2 minutes, add the pork tenderloin to the pot and sear for about 3 minutes. Use tongs or a spatula to flip the tenderloin to the other side. Sear for another 2-3 minutes on this side.

3 Use the tongs to remove the tenderloin from the pot and place it on a plate. Press the "Keep Warm/Cancel" button.

4 Add the garlic to the pot and cook for 1-2 minutes. Pour the apple juice, balsamic vinegar and salt into the pot. Stir together and scrape at the bottom of the pot with the spatula to remove any browned bits. These add great flavor!

5 Sprinkle a pinch of the rosemary and thyme onto the pork tenderloin then add the rest to the pot. Add the apples and stir the whole mixture together.

Dinner - Pork

6 Place the pork tenderloin back in the pot and nestle it into the apple mixture.

7 Close the lid and make sure the steam vent is in the sealed position.

8 Press the "Manual" button and then press the "Pressure" button to adjust to low pressure. Set the timer for 2 minutes.

9 When the timer beeps after 2 minutes, allow the pressure to naturally release for 15 minutes. Then flip the valve to venting and release any remaining pressure.

10 Use your tongs to remove the tenderloin to a clean plate. Press the "Sauté" button on your Instant Pot®.

11 Add the butter and honey to the pot with the apples and stir together.

12 In a small bowl, mix together the cornstarch and water until the cornstarch has dissolved completely. Pour this mixture into the pot with the apples. This will help to thicken the sauce.

13 When the sauce has reached desired thickness, Turn off the Instant Pot®.

14 Slice the pork and served with the balsamic apple sauce as a topping.

Tasty Tip

If you don't mind peeling and dicing the apples, be sure to add 3 apples to this dish. Two is fine, but adding three means there is just that much more to eat when it is done cooking. The balsamic apple sauce is the best part of this recipe!

Tip for Success

If you don't feel comfortable searing the pork in Step 2, you can skip this step. Searing the meat adds great flavor, but it's not mandatory. Plus the balsamic apple sauce will add plenty of yumminess to the dish!

"YOU CAN BE A BIG PIG, TOO" KALUA PORK

Kalua pork is a Hawaiian cooking method that uses an imu or underground fire pit to cook the pork all day. The result is a delicious, flavorful and incredibly tender piece of pork. However, not many kids have an imu in their backyard, so using the Instant Pot® gets the tenderness and the flavor without the long wait.

Serves: 8

What You Need:
- 3 slices of bacon
- 5 pound bone-in pork shoulder roast
- 1 1/2 tablespoons Red Hawaiian coarse sea salt
- 1 cup water
- 1 cabbage, core removed and sliced into 6 wedges (optional)

Tools:
- Tongs

Tongs

How You Make It:

1 Press the "Sauté" button on the Instant Pot® and add the bacon pieces to the bottom of the pot. Fry the bacon until it is cooked, flipping once during the cooking process.

2 When the bacon is cooked, but not too crispy, remove the bacon from the pot and place on a paper towel to drain the grease.

3 Have a grown-up help you slice the pork shoulder into three sections. Try to get the sections pretty close to the same size. One will have the bone in it.

4 Sprinkle the Hawaiian salt over all three sections of meat.

5 Add 1 cup of water to the inner pot of the pressure cooker. Place the salted meat into the pot. Add the bacon to the top of the pork.

6 Close the lid and be sure the steam vent is sealed. Press the "Manual" button and set the timer for 90 minutes.

Dinner - Pork

7 When the timer beeps after 90 minutes, let the pressure release naturally until the silver valve has dropped down. This will take about 15 minutes. Then carefully remove the lid.

8 Use tongs to remove the meat from the pot and place it in a large bowl. Remove and discard the bone. The pork will be very tender and should shred easily if you want to shred it.

9 If you want to cook cabbage, add the cabbage sections to the liquid in the pot. Seal the steam vent and close the lid on the pot. Press the "Manual" button and set the timer for 2 minutes.

10 When the timer beeps after 2 minutes, open the steam vent and quick release the pressure. Remove the lid and use tongs to lift the cabbage out of the pot.

11 Place the cabbage on a serving plate and top with a big helping of the pork.

Tip for Success

If you have a smaller pork shoulder, just plan on 3/4 teaspoon of Hawaiian salt per pound. You don't want to use more than this or your meat will be too salty!

BABY BACK RIBS

Did you know the Instant Pot® makes barbecue ribs that are falling off the bone tender? Yum! Serve these up with extra sauce and lots of napkins because it can get really messy eating these delicious ribs!

Serves: 4

What You Need:
- 1 rack baby back ribs
- 1/4 cup brown sugar
- 2 tablespoons chili powder
- 2 teaspoons dried parsley
- 1 teaspoon salt
- 1 teaspoon pepper
- 1 teaspoon garlic powder
- 1 teaspoon onion powder
- 1 teaspoon cumin
- 1 cup water
- 1/2 cup apple cider vinegar
- 1/4 teaspoon liquid smoke
- 1/2 cup barbecue sauce

Tools:
- Trivet
- Tongs

How You Make It:

1 Ask an adult for help removing the silver membrane from the baby back ribs. This is the silvery-white lining on one side of the ribs. Use a butter knife to loosen it, then slowly pull it until it comes completely off.

2 Mix together the brown sugar, chili powder, parsley, salt, pepper, garlic powder, cumin and onion powder. This is the dry rub. Now coat both sides of the ribs with the dry rub.

3 Pour the water, apple cider vinegar and liquid smoke in the bottom of the Instant Pot®. Place the trivet in the pot. Place the ribs in the pot on top of the trivet, wrapping the ribs along the pot.

4 Close the lid and be sure the steam vent is in the closed position. Press the "Manual" button and set the timer for 25 minutes.

Dinner - Pork

5 When the timer beeps after 25 minutes, allow the pressure to release naturally for at least 10 minutes. Then you can flip open the steam vent to release any remaining pressure.

6 Use tongs to remove the ribs from the pot and place on a large serving plate. Coat with your favorite barbecue sauce and serve with extra sauce on the side.

LEMON SNICKETY SALMON

Salmon is a great source of protein with many health benefits. This includes that it's loaded with Omega 3 Fatty Acids. Those are super good for you! Cooking the salmon in the Instant Pot® steams it so it doesn't get tough or chewy.

Serves: 2

What You Need:
- 2 (4 ounce) salmon fillets, thawed
- 1/2 lemon
- Pinch of salt
- Pinch of ground black pepper
- Rosemary or Dill, fresh sprigs
- 2 cups water (for bottom of the Inner Pot)

Tools:
- 2 Pieces of Tinfoil, 12 inches each
- Trivet
- Tongs
- Cooking Spray

Tongs

Trivet

How You Make It:

1 Spray one side of each tinfoil piece with the cooking spray. Place a salmon fillet, skin side down in the middle of each piece of tinfoil.

2 Add a pinch of salt and pepper to each piece of fish. Top the fish with a sprig of dill or rosemary.

Dinner - Seafood

3 Cut two slices (about 1/4 inch each slice) from a lemon. Give a quick squeeze of the remaining lemon to dribble a little lemon juice on each piece of salmon. Place the lemon slices on top of the salmon fillets.

4 Fold the tinfoil up on all sides, creating a sealed packet for the fish.

5 Pour 2 cups of water into the bottom of the inner pot of the pressure cooker. Place the trivet in the pot and put both sealed packets on top of the trivet. Secure the lid and close the steam vent.

6 Press the "Manual" button and set the timer for 7 minutes. When the cook time is complete, open the steam valve to quick release the pressure.

7 Use tongs to carefully lift the packets out of the pot. Open the packets and transfer the fish to plates for serving.

Tip for Success

When you open up the packets, the fish meat should flake off easily with a fork. If it doesn't, it will need an additional 1-2 minutes of cooking time. Bigger pieces of fish than the 4 ounces suggested will need longer to cook.

PEEL-AND-EAT SHRIMP

Our family loves going to the beach and eating fresh seafood. This is one our favorite recipes. This shrimp is cooked perfectly with just the right amount of seasoning.

Serves: 4

What You Need:
- 1-1.5 pounds shell-on large raw shrimp
- 1/2 lemon
- 1 tablespoon butter
- 2-3 tablespoons Old Bay Seasoning
- 6 cups water

How You Make It:

1 Pour 6 cups of water into the inner pot of your pressure cooker. Stir in the butter and the Old Bay Seasoning.

2 Squeeze the juice out of half a lemon into the pot and then throw the peel from that half into the pot as well.

3 Add the shrimp. Secure the lid and be sure the steam vent is closed.

4 Press the "Manual" button and set the timer for 2 minutes.

5 When the timer beeps after 2 minutes, immediately release the pressure by opening the steam vent.

6 Use a slotted spoon to remove the shrimp.

7 These shrimp are great served warm or cold. To serve cool, transfer them to a large bowl of ice water. After 5-10 minutes, remove the shrimp from the ice water and transfer to a bowl.

8 Serve warm or cold with cocktail sauce or melted butter.

Dinner - seafood

Tasty Tip

Sprinkle 1-2 teaspoons of Old Bay Seasoning onto the shrimp before serving. The seasoning will add great flavor to your fingers as you peel and eat your shrimp!

SHRIMP JAMBALAYA (HAVE BIG FUN ON THE BAYOU!)

Jambalaya is a dish that originated in Louisiana and is a classic Cajun dish. Traditionally it is several types of meat and vegetables all cooked together with rice in a tomato sauce. Ca c'est bon! (Cajun for "It's GOOD!")

Serves: 4-6

What You Need:
- 2 tablespoons olive oil
- 12 ounces of Andouille sausage, cut into 1/2 inch slices
- 1 onion, diced
- 1 bell pepper, de-seeded and diced
- 1 stalk celery, diced
- 3 teaspoons garlic, minced
- 2 teaspoons Cajun seasoning
- 1/4 teaspoon ground thyme
- 1 cup long-grain white rice
- 1 (14.5 ounce) can diced tomatoes, with juice
- 1 1/2 cups chicken broth, low sodium
- 1/2 teaspoon salt
- 12 ounces medium sized cooked shrimp
- 4 scallions, sliced into 1/4 inch pieces

Dinner - Seafood

How You Make It:

1 Add the olive oil to the inner pot of the Instant Pot® and press the "Sauté" button. When the oil is hot, add the sausage slices and cook for about two minutes, until lightly browned on both sides. Use a slotted spoon or spatula to remove the sausage and place on a paper towel-lined plate.

2 Add to the pot the onion, bell pepper and celery and cook for 3-5 minutes, until the vegetables are beginning to soften. Add the garlic and cook one minute longer.

3 Pour in the rice, cajun seasoning and thyme. Stir well to coat the rice in the oil and the seasonings. Press the "Keep Warm/Cancel" button.

4 Pour in the chicken broth, tomatoes and the salt. Stir gently. Close the lid and lock the steam valve.

5 Press the "Manual" button and adjust the cooking timer for 8 minutes.

6 When the timer beeps after 8 minutes, allow the pressure to release naturally for 5 minutes. Then open the steam valve and release the pressure.

7 Stir the rice mixture. Add the sausage, shrimp and scallions to the pot and stir. Close the lid on the pot again and allow to sit for 5 minutes. The heat from the pot will warm the shrimp and sausage.

8 When the shrimp and sausage are warm, remove the lid and stir. Serve with cornbread and a dash of hot sauce if desired.

VOLCANO CHOCOLATE LAVA CAKES

These little cakes have a hidden surprise- gooey chocolate that comes gushing out when you cut into the cake! These cakes make a GREAT treat.

Serves: Makes four 6-ounce cakes

What You Need:
- 1 cup butter (1stick)
- 1 cup semi-sweet chocolate chips
- 1 cup powdered sugar
- 3 eggs
- 1 egg yolk
- 1 tablespoon Vanilla extract
- 6 tablespoons flour

Tools:
- Four 6-ounce Ramekins
- Trivet
- Cooking Spray

Trivet

How You Make It:

1 Place the butter and the chocolate chips in a microwave-safe bowl. Microwave for 30 seconds and stir. Repeat this until the chocolate is melted and smooth.

2 Pour in the powder sugar and mix until well blended.

3 Crack the eggs into the chocolate mixture. Add the yolk of one egg. Stir well.

4 Add the vanilla extract and the flour and blend until the mixture is smooth and creamy.

5 Spray the ramekins with cooking spray. Be sure to get the spray on the sides as well as the bottom.

6 Divide the batter equally into the ramekins.

7 Pour 1 cup of water into the inner pot of the Instant Pot®. Place the trivet inside the pot. Put three ramekins on the trivet. Carefully balance the fourth ramekin on top of the other three.

8 Place the lid on the Instant Pot® and secure it tightly. Be sure that the steam valve is closed.

Desserts

9 Press the "Manual" button and adjust the timer to 8-9 minutes. (8 minutes will give you a really gooey center of the cake. Cooking for 9 minutes will make your cake a little more firm. Chose what you like best!)

10 When the timer beeps and the cooking time is over, flip the steam valve carefully to quick release the pressure.

11 Open the lid and use oven mitts to remove the ramekins. Everything will be hot.

12 Run a dull knife between the edge of the ramekin and the cake to loosen the cake. Turn the bowl upside down on a plate and the cake should fall out.

13 For an extra treat, top with ice cream or berries. Cut into your cake and watch the chocolate lava come spilling out. Careful, its hot!

Tip for Success

If you use a larger or smaller ramekin, adjust the cooking time so your cakes turn out perfect. If using smaller ramekins, the cakes may take a minute or two less to cook. Larger ramekins may take a minute or two longer.

AWESOME APPLE DUMPLINGS

These little apple slices are wrapped in dough and cooked in a sweet sauce. Serve with a scoop of vanilla ice cream or a bit of caramel sauce.

Serves: makes 8 small dumplings

What You Need:
- 1 (8 ounce) can crescent rolls
- 2 medium apples, peeled, cored and diced
- 4 tablespoons butter
- 1/2 cup brown sugar
- 1/2 teaspoon vanilla extract
- 1 teaspoon ground cinnamon
- pinch nutmeg
- 3/4 cup apple juice
- Cooking spray

How You Make It:

1 Prepare your apples by peeling, removing the core and dicing into small pieces.

2 Unroll the crescent rolls and spread flat. In each crescent roll, place about 2-3 tablespoons of diced apple. Roll the crescent roll up with the apple in the middle. Repeat with all the crescent rolls, saving any leftover apple pieces.

3 Spray the inner pot of your pressure cooker with cooking spray. Press the "Sauté" button.

4 Add the butter and allow it to melt. Stir in the sugar, cinnamon, nutmeg and vanilla. Press the "Keep Warm/Cancel" button.

5 Place the dumplings into the butter mixture, side by side. Pour the apple juice gently on the sides and in between the dumplings. Add any leftover apple pieces to the pot now.

6 Close the lid and be sure the steam vent is sealed.

7 Press the "Manual" button and set the cook time for 10 minutes.

Desserts

Tasty Tip

The dough for the dumplings doesn't get crispy in the Instant Pot®. If you like crispy dumplings, transfer them to a baking dish and broil them for a few minutes in the oven. Serve your apple dumplings with a scoop of vanilla ice cream!

8 When the timer beeps after 10 minutes, allow the pressure to release naturally for another 10 minutes. Then open the steam vent to release any remaining pressure and open the lid.

9 Use a large spoon to remove the dumplings and top with the cooking sauce.

OREO CHEESECAKE

This dessert takes a bit of work, but wow is it worth it. This is one of the best things your Instant Pot® can make! Although the springform pan is little, this cake is very thick and rich so it should serve 6-8 people.

Serves: 6-8

What You Need:

Crust:
- 12 Oreos, crushed into fine crumbs
- 2 tablespoons butter, melted

Cheesecake:
- 16 ounces of cream cheese, room temperature
- 1/2 cup, plus 1 tablespoon white sugar
- 2 large eggs, room temperature
- 1 tablespoon flour
- 1/4 cup heavy cream
- 2 teaspoons vanilla extract
- 8 Oreos, coarsely chopped

Topping: (optional)
- 8 whole Oreos, coarsely chopped
- chocolate sauce, for drizzling

Tools:
- 7 Inch Springform Pan
- Trivet
- Stand Mixer or Hand Mixer
- Cooking Spray
- Foil for Sling

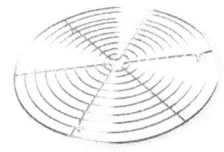
Trivet

How You Make It:

1 Prepare a 7 inch springform pan by spraying the inside with cooking spray. Pour 2 cups of water into the inner pot of the pressure cooker and place the trivet in the pot.

2 To prepare the crust, mix together the Oreo cookie crumbs with 2 tablespoons of melted butter. Mix it so the crumbs become a little sticky, then pour the crumbs into the bottom of the springform pan. Use your fingers to press the crumbs into the bottom and up the sides about 1 inch of the pan, forming a crust for the cheesecake.

Desserts

3 Place the crust in the freezer while you mix together the cheesecake.

4 To make the cheesecake, you will need a stand mixer or an electric hand mixer. Use the mixer to beat the cream cheese until it is creamy. Add the sugar and beat until smooth. Add the eggs, one at a time beating in between. You will want to scrape the sides of the bowl with a spatula to make sure everything becomes well blended.

5 Finally, add in the flour, heavy cream, and vanilla and mix until creamy and smooth.

6 Dump in the chopped Oreos and stir gently. Pour the batter into the prepared springform pan crust.

7 Cover the pan with a piece of tinfoil to prevent condensation from dripping on the cheesecake.

8 Create a sling by taking a piece of foil 20 inches long and folding it in half lengthwise twice. See page 11 for instructions.)

9 Set the sling into the inner pot of the pressure cooker and place it on the trivet so that the "handles" come up the side of the pot and then carefully lower the springform pan into the pot on top of the sling. Close the lid and make sure the steam vent is sealed.

10 Press the "Manual" button and set the cook time for 35 minutes.

11 When the timer beeps after 35 minutes, allow the pressure to release naturally for 10 minutes. Then open the steam vent to release any remaining pressure. Open the pot carefully.

12 Use the sling to carefully lift the cheesecake onto the counter. (You may want a grownup to help you.) Pull out the hot trivet and set the pan on the trivet to allow it to cool.

13 When the cheesecake has cooled, place it in the refrigerator to chill for 6-8 hours or overnight before serving.

14 To serve, you may want to top it with chopped Oreos and a light drizzle of chocolate sauce.

EASY BREEZY PEACH PIE

Peach pie in an instant! This recipe is a favorite in our house and is super easy to make.

Serves: 2

What You Need:
- 1 ripe peach
- 1/2 teaspoon butter
- 3 teaspoons brown sugar
- 1/8 teaspoon ground cinnamon
- 1 graham cracker, chopped
- 2 scoops vanilla ice cream

Tools:
- 2 Ramekins
- Spoon or Melon baller
- Trivet

Trivet

Ramekin

How You Make It:

1. Wash and dry the peach and cut it in half. Remove the pit. Use a spoon or melon baller to help remove the pit and make the pit indention just a little bigger. This will create a "bowl" for the butter and sugar. Place each peach half into a ramekin, "bowl" side up.

2. Mix together the brown sugar and cinnamon.

3. Divide the butter, adding 1/4 teaspoon to the "bowl" of each peach. Then divide the sugar mixture adding it to the top of the peach.

4. Add 2 cups of water to the inner pot of the Instant Pot® and place in the trivet. Add the ramekins to the inner pot on top of the trivet. Close the lid and the steam vent.

5. Press the "Manual" button and adjust the timer to 5-7 minutes. When the timer beeps after the cook time, allow the pressure to reduce naturally for five minutes. Then open the steam vent and release the pressure. (Five minutes for warm, but more firm peaches or 7 minutes for pie filling peaches.)

Desserts

6 Carefully open the lid and use oven mitts to remove the ramekins. Allow the ramekins to cool for 5-10 minutes as they will be hot!

7 The peach will be mushy so use a spoon to gently stir and mix with the juices. Top each peach with half a crumbled graham cracker. Add a scoop of vanilla ice cream and serve. Delicious!

FUDGY PEANUT BUTTER BROWNIES

If you like chocolate and peanut butter together then this is the recipe for you. If you don't like peanut butter, you can leave it out of the recipe and the brownies will still be delicious.

Serves: 6

What You Need:
- 5 tablespoons melted butter
- 1/4 cup unsweetened cocoa powder
- 1 cup sugar
- 3/4 cup flour
- 1/2 teaspoon vanilla extract
- 3/4 teaspoon baking powder
- 2 eggs
- 3 tablespoons chocolate chips
- 4 teaspoons creamy peanut butter
- 1 1/2 cups water (For the bottom of the inner pot)

Tools:
- 6 Inch Springform Pan
- Trivet
- Cooking Spray
- Aluminum Foil

How You Make It:

1 In a medium mixing bowl, blend together the cocoa powder, sugar, flour and baking powder. Pour in the melted butter and vanilla extract, then add the eggs. Stir with a mixing spoon until all ingredients are well blended.

2 Add the chocolate chips and mix into the batter.

3 Spray a 6 inch springform pan with cooking spray. Pour the batter into the pan.

4 Drop 4 teaspoons of creamy peanut butter in four separate spaces on top of the batter. Use a spoon to lightly cover the peanut butter with the batter and swirl it into the batter a little bit. It doesn't have to be perfect, it will be delicious either way!

5 Pour 1 1/2 cups of water into the inner pot of the pressure cooker and put the trivet in.

6 Cover the top of the springform pan with aluminum foil to prevent water from dripping on the brownies.

Desserts

7 Create a foil sling (see page 11 for details on this) and lower the pan onto the trivet in the pressure cooker. Close the lid and be sure the steam vent is in the sealed position.

8 Press the "Manual" button and set the timer for 50 minutes.

9 When the timer beeps after 50 minutes, allow the pressure to release naturally for 5 minutes, then open the steam vent to release any remaining pressure.

10 Use the sling to remove the pan from the inner pot. Allow to cool for several minutes before opening the springform pan.

11 Slice and serve while they are still warm.

"MONKEYING AROUND" MONKEY BREAD

Monkey bread is fun to make and even better to eat! If you want to make the edges crispy after they have cooked in the Instant Pot®, ask a grownup to help you use the oven broiler for just a few minutes. If you want to use all the biscuits to make monkey bread, just work in batches.

Serves: 2

What You Need:
- 1 (7.5 ounce) package canned biscuits (you will only need 4 of the 10 biscuits)
- 3 tablespoons white sugar
- 1/2 teaspoon ground cinnamon
- 2 tablespoons butter, melted
- 2 tablespoons brown sugar
- 1 cup water

Tools:
- Trivet
- 2 Ramekins
- Cooking Spray
- Oven Mitt

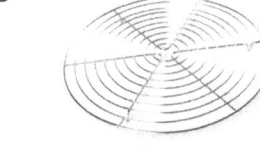
Trivet

Ramekin

How You Make It:

1 Prepare the ramekins by spraying them lightly with cooking spray.

2 Open the package of biscuits and separate 4 biscuits to use for the Monkey Bread. Bake the remaining biscuits or wrap in plastic wrap to use later.

3 Use scissors or a pizza cutter to divide each biscuit into 4 sections. You should now have 16 small pieces of dough.

4 In a small bowl, mix together the white sugar and the ground cinnamon. Drop several pieces of dough into the sugar mixture and coat completely.

5 Place the sugar-coated pieces of dough into the ramekins, eight pieces per ramekin.

6 Pour 1 cup water into the bottom of the inner pot of the pressure cooker and place the trivet into the pot.

Desserts

7 Set the ramekins on top of the trivet and close the lid. Be sure the steam vent is in the sealed position.

8 Press the "Manual" button and set the timer for 20 minutes.

9 When the cooking time is complete, quick release the pressure and carefully open the lid.

10 Use oven mitts to remove the ramekins. Allow to cool slightly, then turn the ramekins over on a plate to remove the monkey bread.

11 If you like, sprinkle a little of the remaining cinnamon-sugar mixture over the monkey bread before serving. It's delicious served with a small scoop of vanilla ice cream on the side or on top!

INDEX

"Monkeying Around" Monkey Bread, 124
"Ooh La La!" French Toast Bake, 30
acorn squash, 48
Acorn Squash with Brown Sugar and Butter, 48
Alfredo sauce, 72
apple, 24, 28, 102, 116
Apple Cinnamon Steel Cut Oats, 24
Apple Dumpling Gang Apple Dumplings, 116
artichoke hearts, 38
asparagus, 54
Baby Back Ribs, 106
bacon, 44, 58, 104
Baked Potato Heads, 64
barbecue sauce, 78, 80, 98, 106
BBQ Chicken Sliders, 80
beans, 88
beef broth, 86, 88, 90
Beef Stroganoff, 90
berries, 26
Berry Good Triple Berry Oatmeal, 26
Big Kid Beef and Broccoli, 96
biscuits, 124
Blissful & "Bacony" Green Beans, 44
bread, 30, 62

broccoli, 96
Buffalo Chicken Dip, 36
cabbage, 104
carrots, 46, 52, 56, 84, 86
celery, 52, 56, 84, 112
cheddar cheese, 20, 36, 64, 66, 72
Cheesy Stuffed Chicken in Alfredo Sauce, 72
Cheesy Vegetable Risotto, 54
chicken breasts, 36, 58, 62, 70, 72, 74, 78, 80, 84, 98, 112
chicken broth, 38, 52, 54, 56, 66, 70, 80, 84, 98, 112
Chicken Corn Chowder, 58
Chicken Noodle "Sick Day" Soup, 84
Chicken Salad Sandwiches, 62
chicken stock, 58, 74, 76, 98, 100
Chicken Tacos (Dragon Approved), 70
chicken wings, 34
Chili sauce, 88
chocolate chips, 30, 114, 122
Cocktail Meatballs, 32
corn, 42, 58
Corn-errific Corn on the Cob, 21
Country Style Boneless Pork Ribs, 98
cranberry sauce, 32

Creamy Dreamy Tomato Soup, 60
Criss Cross Applesauce, 28
Easy Breezy Peach Pie, 120
egg noddles, 84
eggs, 20, 22, 30, 114, 122
Fudgy Peanut Butter Brownies, 122
garbanzo beans, 40
grapes, 62
Greek yogurt, 64
green beans, 44
ground beef, 86, 88, 92, 94
ham, 20, 56
heavy whipping cream, 58
honey, 34, 46, 74, 100, 102
Honey Cinnamon Kissed Carrot Candy, 46
Honey Garlic Chicken Wings, 34
hot dogs, 68
Hummus is Yummus!, 40
ice cream, 120
Italian Dressing Seasoning, 38
Kalua Pork, 104
lemon, 40, 54, 62, 76, 108
Lemon Snickety Salmon, 108
Macaroni and Cheese, Please!, 66
Magnificent Meatloaf Muffins, 94
Mashed Potatoes, Not Couch Potatoes, 50
meatballs, 32
mushrooms, 90
oats, 26, 94
Oreo Cheesecake, 118
peanut butter, 122
peas, 52, 56
Peel-and-Eat Shrimp, 110
pesto, 82
pineapple, 78

Pineapple Chicken, 78
Pork Tenderloin in Balsamic Apple Sauce, 102
potatoes, 50, 58, 64
Presto Pesto Chicken Packets, 82
Princess and the Split Pea Soup, 56
Pulled Pork in BBQ Sauce, 100
Quack-tastic Hard Boiled Eggs, 22
ranch dip seasoning, 36
rice, 52, 54
Rice Pilaf, 52
roast beef, 96
Rosemary Lemon "Big Ole" Whole Chicken, 76
salsa, 64
sausage, 112
shredded cheddar cheese, 36
shredded cheese, 20
shredded Parmesan Cheese, 38
Shrimp Jambalaya, 112
Sloppy Joe, Slop Sloppy Joe, 86
soy sauce, 34, 74, 96
Spaghetti, 92
spinach, 38
Spinach Artichoke Dip, 38
Step Right Up, Get Yer Hot Dogs!, 68
Sweet and Sassy Honey Chicken, 74
syrup, 48
Volcano Chocolate Lava Cakes, 114
Willy Nilly Chili, 88

www.ingramcontent.com/pod-product-compliance
Lightning Source LLC
Chambersburg PA
CBHW051348110526
44591CB00025B/2937